Quadrille, Penguin Random House UK,
One Embassy Gardens, 8 Viaduct Gardens,
London SW11 7BW

Quadrille Publishing Limited is part of the Penguin Random House group of companies whose addresses can be found at global.penguinrandomhouse.com

Published by Quadrille in 2025

www.penguin.co.uk

A CIP catalogue record for this book is available from the British Library

ISBN 978 1 83783 428 0
10 9 8 7 6 5 4 3 2 1

Managing Director Sarah Lavelle
Editorial Director Harriet Butt
Assistant Editor Oreolu Grillo
Project Editor Marie Clayton
Design and Art Direction Gemma Hayden
Photography Kim Lightbody
Prop Stylist Milly Bruce
Model Katherine Beckwith
Head of Production Stephen Lang
Production Manager Sabeena Atchia

Color reproduction by FI

Printed in China by C&C Offset Printing Co. Ltd

The authorized representative in the EEA is Penguin Random House Ireland, Morrison Chambers, 32 Nassau Street, Dublin D02 YH68.

Penguin Random House is committed to a sustainable future for our business, our readers and our planet. This book is made from Forest Stewardship Council® certified paper.

The Handmade Home

21 Simple Sewing Projects for Your Home

Arounna Khounnoraj

Photography by Kim Lightbody

contents

introduction

It was always my goal to open a bricks-and-mortar shop. A place where I could house my studio and production work, but also a place where I could show all the textiles and home goods that I made, all thoughtfully arranged with a curator's touch. And a place where I could connect with customers and friends – helping to create a community of like-minded people, sharing a belief in the importance of handmade things. Reflecting back on those times, it's not without amusement that I realize, as a maker, I've spent most of my career creating things for other people. But in doing so I've also benefited. In my house there is no shortage of the things I make – my studio one-offs, experiments and fully realized products are all part of my environment. But it is more than just happenstance that I live with my work; it is also a matter of choice. I've come to understand that the things we live with reflect our ideas and values, how we think and how we want to live. And making allows you to create an environment that is truly your own.

Of course this is not a new idea. For generations past, making had been a large part of everyday life. If you needed something you would make it, quite often with materials that you had on hand. Many homes engaged in the cycle of making, using, and mending. But more recently, it has been far too easy to accept our consumer culture with its endless array of objects and design choices that seem generic and always the same. And, too, overlook the costs to our environment that are inherent to mass production and consumption. But it doesn't have to be like this.

In my experience I've found that making, and living with the things you make, can be gratifying in so many ways. Expressing yourself in your own creations allows you to add your own personality, ideas, and aesthetic choices in whatever way you wish. And by working economically and adopting a "use what you have" approach, it's always amazing what you can do with less. Connecting with your home while making considered design decisions gives you creative opportunities that are beneficial for both your home and our world. It's also been my experience as a teacher that, with a few examples for inspiration, some guidance, and technique, anyone can be a maker and make beautiful items for themselves and their home.

With this in mind, my goal with this book was to gather a collection of projects for every room in your home – bedroom, kitchen, living room, and anywhere in between. Projects for home goods suitable for any space and any activity. But I should mention a couple of common themes that to my mind serve to unify this collection: firstly, it's my preference to look for beauty in simplicity, in natural fabric, and organic textures – in assemblages and patchworks that are visually modern, but with hand-made techniques that provide a hint of tradition. And secondly, my love for things that are useful, for the tabletop, to organize and store, and to make our favorite places comfortable. The things that every home can never have enough of.

I hope you will see this as more than just a collection of sewing projects, and instead as a book to expand your making skills while thinking creatively about the things we live with. And a book to make your home your own.

how to use this book

There are certain basic expectations that we have for workbooks: providing all the necessary information along with clear and concise steps to achieve the goals of each project. But as important as that information is, in many ways that is just the start. Along with instructions, it's my hope that these projects will broaden your skills and introduce new techniques suitable for sewing projects. But even more, I hope to inspire you – to make your own work, become comfortable in your own decision making, and continue into a life of creativity.

But inspiration comes in different ways for different makers. And because I see this as a book that will keep all skill levels busy, there are a few things to bear in mind. Some prefer to learn by following along closely to the instructions I've provided, step-by-step, moving forward with a clear destination in mind. Others seem to enjoy the creative opportunities that come from making discoveries along the way.

In either case, I have provided all the information each project will need, along with photographs, drawings, and step by step instructions. An additional section specifically addresses tools and materials, and there are some necessary sewing techniques and construction methods, such as how to join fabric with different seams and ways to create hems, which will serve as a reference as you work. I've used sewing methods that anyone can do without specialized skills or equipment. While I use hand work wherever it is necessary, occasionally I will use a sewing machine for expediency. However, there is no reason why hand work alone won't be perfectly fine.

I've sourced a variety of tools, materials, and threads from some of my favorite shops and have listed them alongside each project, chosen with accessibility in mind. But that said, I would also emphasize that to use different materials, something that you prefer or that speaks to you in a different way, is quite often the better choice. So, feel free to make changes as you see fit. I also encourage you to use materials or items that you may already have on hand. I am forever searching through my stash looking for the right piece of fabric or color of thread and am always pleasantly surprised when I find something perfect. And to be honest, this sort of thinking is something I definitely want to promote – it's economical, creates less waste, and pushes us to think creatively with what we have, finding new ideas that we may not have otherwise thought of.

Likewise, keep in mind that there are always design decisions that are open to interpretation or modification. After all, creativity is full of possibilities. When I work I tend to think organically – I let some ideas guide me in a specific direction, but also feel the freedom to try alternatives, change the look of something or even add my favorite techniques. I certainly welcome you to do the same.

tools and materials

Most of us have a home sewing kit that provides a few of the basic tools for sewing, and it's sometimes amazing how much can be done with so little. But there are definitely some additions to that will make working easier and will open our making to so much potential. A lot of my work consists of hand sewing, because there are many techniques and stitches that can only be done by hand. But equally, I consider machine sewing to be an important part of the process; it will speed your work and give consistent results. This list of materials is of those that I consider essential for both hand and machine sewing.

Hand-sewing needles

Needles will be your most used tool for virtually everything, so having a quality and comfortable needle is very important. While there are many types of needles for specific types of textile work, I find that there just a few that are essential for hand sewing.

Sharps (1)

Sharps are all purpose hand-sewing needles and are perfectly suited for sewing fabric together. They tend to be sharper and thinner than other types of needles in order to go through layers of cloth easily. With some exceptions, they are sized from 1 to 12, with 1 being the largest and 12 the smallest. The larger sizes are longer with larger eyes and work well for thicker materials, while the mid-range sizes, 5 to 9, are perfect for light to medium weight fabrics. I use sharps that are around size 5 – they are well sized for the average fabric I use, and at 1½in (4cm) in length, I find them comfortable to hold.

Sashiko (2)

These are Japanese needles typically used for making running stitches. They are thicker with larger eyes than standard sharps, allowing them to accommodate thicker thread, and are longer so they can gather several stitches at a time before being pulled through the fabric. Like sharps, they will easily go through even heavy material. Because you can load the needle, sewing with Sashiko needles is fast and makes for neat and concise stitches. They come in a variety of lengths, with the longer ones better suited to straight lines and the smaller for curved lines.

Darning needles (3)

Darning needles are larger than typical sewing needles with a couple of important differences. They have large eyes to accommodate heavier threads and yarns, and dull rounded tips so they can weave within existing fabrics, such as knits, without catching or splitting any thread or yarn along the way. As the name suggests, this makes them more suitable for mending, weaving, and some embroidery than actual sewing – but they have a place when stitching into existing fabrics such as sweaters repurposed into sewing projects, or when using materials with large open weaves. They come in an array of sizes that differ in length, shaft width, and eye size.

1
4
13
11
20
17
11
18
9
6
19
7
8
14
16
13
10
5
12
RotaTrim A3
KAI
5028
3
2
15

Needle storage (4)

Keeping needles organized is important because they can be easily damaged or dulled and, of course, because they are easy to lose. I store my needles in a needle book or a tubular case so they are safe, organized, and I always know where they are. And because hand sewing can be done anywhere, needle books and containers let us travel without worrying about where our favorite needles are.

Needle threader (5)

Hand sewing means that you will be threading your needle for every line of stitches you make, and we all know that can sometimes be tricky given needles with tiny eyes and uncooperative threads. Threaders can help with these difficulties and speed up the process as well, so it's worth having a few handy. There are many different kinds of needle threaders, each with their own advantages. The most basic have a fine wire loop on the end of a holder that is inserted into the eye of the needle, then thread is placed in the loop to be easily pulled through the eye. I also find the ones that look like flat hooks to be good. Try out a few to see which ones you like best.

Measuring tools

Tape measure (6)

Tape measures for sewing are typically flexible so that they can be used for determining the measurements while sewing, but also for taking body dimensions. But a flexible tape measure is equally useful for all other types of sewing too – they are long, easy to use, and convenient to keep near both the cutting table and the sewing machine for both large and more detailed measurements. I like the retractable ones that I can easily slide inside my portable sewing kit.

Grid ruler (7)

Grid rulers are variations on standard rulers but with some important differences. Typically, they are made of clear acrylic so they are transparent, and come in various lengths as well as widths. What makes grid rulers even more useful is that, along with measurements, they are printed with grids and various diagonals for when cutting patterns, repetitions, and pieces that need to accurately fit together such as in quilting. For that reason, grid rulers are often used when cutting with rotary tools. I like to use one that is 6 x 24in (15 x 30cm), but having a smaller 6 x 6in (15 x 15cm) one is also handy.

Marking tools

Marking fabric is a necessary step in creating, constructing, and sewing. Being able to draw directly onto fabric has so many applications – laying out patterns and shapes for cutting, organizing stitch lines or measurements for folds, and for laying down decorative designs across a fabric surface. There are many household items that can be used: pencils for light colored fabric, white or colored pencil crayons for darks, and even markers such as Micro pens that are thin and permanent. But these should only be used where the marks will be hidden within seams or not seen after cutting. Sometimes marks cannot be hidden, but there are many options available. These are a few that I find useful.

Hera markers (8)

These are among my favorites. They are similar to a dull knife, which you glide along the surface of your fabric, either freeform or along the edge of a ruler, leaving a visible, but temporary crease for marking any type of stitch line for seams or quilting. Simply move the ruler to make parallel lines. The creases are visible on most fabrics and colors, and if you change your mind, spritz with a little water to relax the fibers and the creases will disappear.

Water-soluble markers (9)

If you want to make a more visible line for stitching, then water-soluble markers are a great alternative. Similar to a fine marker, they disappear when you apply moisture. These markers work best on lighter colored fabrics.

Tailor's chalk (10)

This is probably one of the oldest ways to mark fabric and create stitch lines; it can be brushed off easily or washed away when finished. I don't use chalk as much as other methods because I find the marks disappear easily when handling the fabric while working, but it is a good solution for darker fabrics or ones that don't crease well.

Securing tools

These are the tools you will use to hold fabric or templates in place before marking or cutting.

Pins/safety pins (11)

Pins may only play a small part in your work but they are always useful, so make sure to have plenty. Straight pins hold layers of cloth together while planning and cutting, and hold fabric in place while sewing – especially useful for machine sewing because you can easily place or remove them while working. Safety pins are good for basting (tacking) larger pieces of fabric on items that might be moved around while you work, such as quilts, or when you prefer to have your work sitting on your lap. As an alternative, you can use a needle and thread to baste down the layers.

Pattern weights (12)

Because fabric and patterns can easily move while working, pattern weights can be really helpful to hold them down on your worktable while cutting. They can also be strategically placed while you plan or before you pin. Store bought weights come in various sizes, weights, and materials, but making them is easy. Just sew up small bags of rice or similar. I also have a small collection of stones that I use.

Cutting tools

There are several options for cutting fabric, so you can choose which best suits the project you are working on.

Scissors/snips (13)

A pair of good scissors is a precious item in any sewing studio and a necessity for all forms of fabric cutting. Find a comfortable pair that works for your hand and use them only for fabric or threads. You might also find it useful to have a clearly marked secondary pair of scissors on standby for other studio tasks and for paper. Snips are small scissors with no handle that are perfectly sized and shaped for cutting small areas and corners, or for cutting threads. Plan to have more than one pair and strategically locate them next to your sewing machine or cutting table.

Rotary knife (14)

A rotary cutter resembles a pizza cutter and makes it easy to cut fabric, or layers of fabric, quickly and efficiently. They are typically used on top of a smooth cutting mat and alongside a ruler or straight edge to hold the fabric in place while cutting. Rotary cutters can cut precise and straight lines of any length, which is sometimes difficult with scissors, making them great additions for cutting lots of fabric and simple shapes – such as in quilting, which requires precise, repetitive cuts.

Cutting mat (15)

A cutting mat is a necessary component used alongside a rotary cutter to protect your work surface and keep your blade sharp. And because they are printed with grids and rulers, they can be used to plan and measure fabric pieces for assembly before accurate cutting with a rotary knife.

Seam ripper (16)

While sewing is about construction, there will always be moments of deconstruction - taking seams apart, redoing a step, or changing our mind and moving in another direction. Seam rippers make it possible. With a tip designed to pick up stitches and a hook blade, these little tools quickly cut through and remove stitching, even in areas that are too small for scissors.

Machines

Sewing machine

Sewing machines are in many ways a cornerstone of a sewing studio. For me, they work alongside hand sewing, doing all the basic tasks that don't require the same attention that hand work needs. Of course, it's always possible to work by hand if that is your preference or if you don't have access to a machine. But there are things that sewing machines excel at: they are fast, helping you complete projects quickly and efficiently, and they offer predictable results. This is especially evident when you have repeated elements to sew, such as when you are piecing fabric together, or when you are working on larger, more complex projects that can be difficult by hand.

A basic machine with the standard set of stitches is all that is needed – just make sure you can change the length of the stitch and work a zigzag stitch. If you occasionally have to sew heavy fabric, you can use a stronger needle and sew at a slower speed. More importantly are attachments that are available with sewing machines, such as the different types of specialized sewing feet. One that I rely on regularly is a zipper foot, which comes in different forms, but makes it possible to sew close to the zipper teeth with perfect results.

Serger / Overlocker

These machines are used to finish raw edges of fabric in order to avoid fraying, and to protect seams due to wear and tear over time. They save time, and create specialized stitches that are usually meant to be hidden from view – on the wrong side or inside items.

I use a serger a lot for items where I don't add a lining, like pillows. If you don't have access to one of these machines, there are a number of alternatives to stabilize edges such as creating wider seam allowances, sewing a hem, or using the zigzag stitch. There are times when I've simply used a bit of fabric glue along the edges of fabric.

Other tools

Wood seam roller (17)

I used to use an iron to flatten my seams while sewing or patching, but that meant going back and forth to the iron and heating it up. Recently I started using a seam roller instead, a cylinder of wood or plastic with a handle used to roll seams flat without heat after you have opened them up. It is especially useful since you can conveniently use it at your sewing machine between steps; having a flat seams helps to keep your work neat. Seam rollers come in different widths but I find the 1in (2.5cm) or 1½in (4cm) ones are good sizes to use.

Thimble (18)

Hand sewing can sometimes be difficult depending on the fabric the number of layers. And when there is a lot to do, it can be tiring. A thimble is another little tool that makes a big difference when trying to sew effectively and comfortably. Common thimbles, typically made of metal, leather, or rubber, fit on the tip of a finger allowing you to push the needle through fabric without stabbing yourself. Sashiko thimbles consist of a ring, worn at the base of the middle finger, with a small coin-like plate used to push long Sashiko needles through fabric with your palm, freeing up your fingertips to load the needle with stitches. I often use rubber thimbles on two fingers to help me grip a needle as I pull it through fabric.

Beeswax (19)

This is another item that helps make hand sewing easier as some threads can be prone to tangles or can be difficult to pull through fabric. Running your thread through beeswax before sewing is a way of conditioning the thread so that it glides through cloth easier with less chance of breaking.

Glue

White glue or glue sticks are handy items for sewing projects when standard methods don't quite apply, or you want a quick solution. I occasionally apply some to a cut edge to stop the fabric from fraying or to baste down pieces of fabric while stitching.

Fabrics

Fabric is the foundation of sewing, and the qualities of fabric we choose informs everything from its functionality and appearance, to how we experience and live with it. There are so many possibilities, and there aren't always clear rights or wrongs when determining what fabric to use. I've learned that many of these qualities are also a matter of personal preference. However, a good place to start is to consider the purpose of the item you are making, because this in turn will provide clues to the needs of the fabric: will the item be subject to more wear and tear or less; is it more important for the fabric to be textured or soft and smooth; opaque or transparent and light; lay flat on a table, or move in the breeze? Many questions like these come down to a few basic qualities – what the fabric is made of, the weight, texture, and feel, and if it is workable for you.

For my homeware projects, I gravitate to natural fabrics, such as cotton and especially linen, usually in medium weights. These fabrics, whether 100 per cent or blends, are typically fairly even-weave in both directions, and are woven with a single strand and a tighter weave. As a result I find them to be the most suitable fabrics for the type of projects I like to sew. They cut well in any direction, the weave is even and full without the gaps of open weave fabrics, they have a balance in weight, and are smooth without too much texture – which means they can be readily printed. And they sew well, by machine or by hand.

Of course, other fabrics catch my eye too – fabrics that stand apart and contrast in some way, for expressive and decorative purposes. And also fabrics that have had a previous life: used or vintage materials from home, such old sheets that can be cut up and used in a different way.

Threads

There are as many types of threads as there are fabric, and determining which to use really depends on the project at hand. When choosing thread for sewing projects I tend to use a quality, all-purpose thread that I can use for both hand sewing and machine sewing. But there are a few things to consider, most notably weight and whether the thread is natural or synthetic.

While I keep cotton threads on hand, for most types of sewing I find threads combined with some polyester to be the best general purpose thread. It offers a good balance between functionality and appearance, is durable, doesn't break easily when sewing, will stand up to wear and tear, and comes in a variety of colors and weights.

If I am sewing a lightweight fabric I tend to use a lighter weight thread, otherwise there may be puckering, and the stitch will be too noticeable. I find 60 wt is a good weight for light to medium fabrics; it is perfect for construction of your items and will not stand out visually. When I do want stitches that are more noticeable, I quite often use a 40 wt thread, which is a little heavier. This thread is great for stitches that you want to highlight, such as in topstitching, but can also be used to reinforce heavier fabric.

Sashiko threads (20)

Sashiko threads are traditional Japanese cotton threads used for hand sewing, such as quilting, joining layers of fabric together (Boro) and for topstitching. They are similar to embroidery floss (thread), being made of thin strands of cotton thread, but are non-divisible and have a more natural matte finish. They come in limited sizes, usually a thin, medium, and heavy weight. I often use Sashiko thread for decorative stitching and for topstitching where I want a stronger and more graphic appearance.

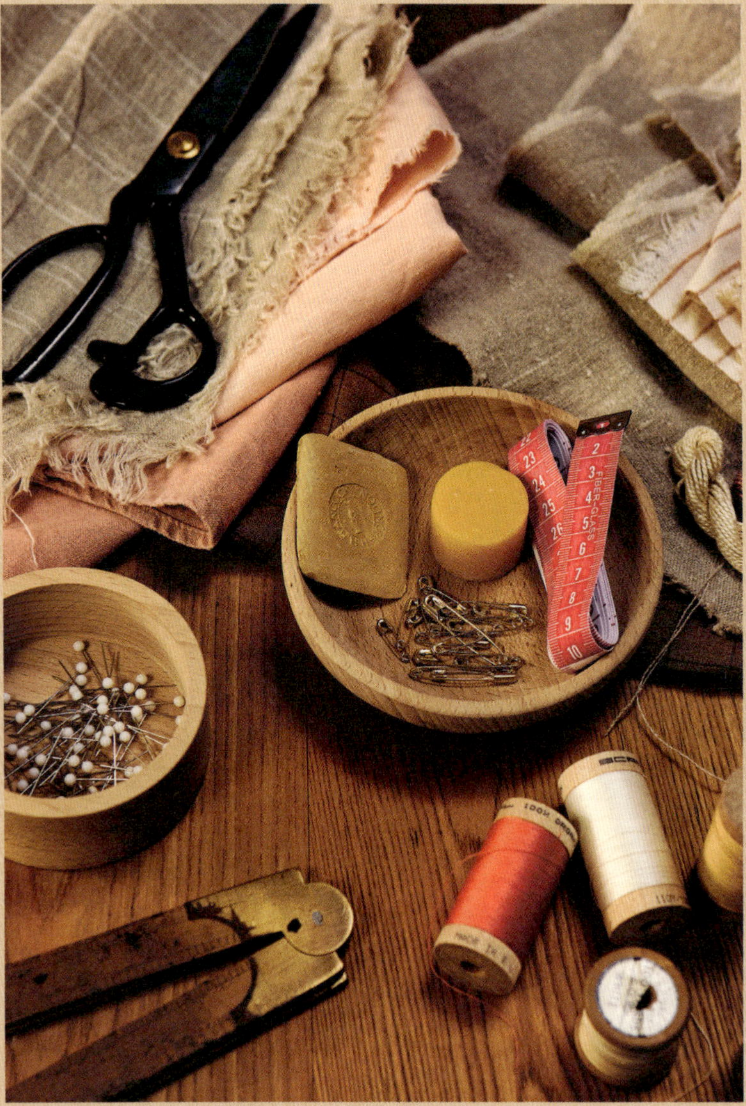

sewing techniques

sewing techniques

A knowledge of sewing techniques can make a real difference in getting the most out of working with textiles. After all, this is what literally holds everything together. Although this is a broad topic, it doesn't have to be daunting. Here are a handful of basic techniques chosen specifically for constructing fabric (and some that double as decorative elements), which will help you achieve wonderful results and can be used over and over for future explorations. Of course, there are countless other techniques and variations, some with highly specific applications, but keep in mind that all sewing techniques and stitches are related to each other, so start here with a good foundation and the rest will come in due course. One note about stitching in particular: as you acquire the skills for each technique and learn how each is used, keep in mind that stitches go well beyond their use as a means to construct. The materials and techniques you choose are visual and textural in their own right – they are elements that are an important part of any design.

Cutting fabric

Before cutting any fabric, first consider how it will be used in any given project. Woven fabric such as most cottons and linens made on a loom, consist of a few basic components: the warp, which are threads running the length of the fabric and form the straight grain; and the weft, which are threads running across from side to side and form the cross grain. On the finished edges of the fabric is the selvage, which always runs parallel to the warp/straight grain. If the selvage is present, you will be able to identify the grain of your fabric.

Typically, it is better to cut patterns oriented along the straight grain because it tends to be more stable with less stretch than the cross grain. For most of the projects in this book you will want to cut with the straight grain. If you want some movement in a certain direction, such as with clothing, you might want to take advantage of the stretch cross grain affords. If your project does not specify either direction, or if your fabric is fairly stable in both directions, then you can cut according to other concerns such as appearance or trying to avoid waste.

A third direction is referred to as the bias, which is at a 45-degree angle to the straight and cross grains. Fabric cut on the bias has considerably more stretch than fabric cut on either grain. Strips of fabric cut on the bias, otherwise known as bias tape, can be easily sewn into curves or around corners.

Basic sewing machine techniques

Straight stitch

This is the most common machine stitch used and is the foundation of the construction of sewn pieces. The machine version of running stitch, a straight stitch is a simple linear element of any length made up of individual stitches with no spaces between them. They appear as a solid line and can be used to attach fabrics together with sewn seams, when sewing appliqué to a surface, or for decoration like topstitching. As with most stitches, it is recommended to back stitch at the beginning and end to ensure that the stitches remain stable.

Zigzag stitch

A zigzag stitch is available on most sewing machines. It consists of a continuous line of back and forth diagonal stitches and is commonly used for finishing and stabilizing the raw edges of fabric if you don't have a serger (overlock) machine. It is also good for sewing stretchy fabrics, such as knitwear or jersey, because it allows the material to stretch, or delicate items like lace where its lack of linearity allows it to blend in. The zigzag also works as a decorative element such as when attaching appliqué, or finishing edges with a graphic pattern. Although each machine is different, zigzag stitch settings typically allow you to experiment by using different stitch lengths and spacing for the zigzags. For example, when spaced tightly together the zigzag stitch mimics a satin stitch which is great for the edges of napkins or table linens. It can also be used to gather fabric when creating ruffles.

Topstitching

As the name implies, topstitching is quite often the final sewn element applied to a project. It typically has a dual purpose of stabilizing edges, hems or seams, but also works as decorative element – a linear or graphic detail meant to be seen on the outside and to visually emphasize your sewing as a whole. Topstitching usually consists of straight stitches on top of the fabric, ¼in (0.6cm) or less from a seam or edge, meant to keep edges clean and crisp with a finished look. For visual effect you might like to use a thread that's a bit heavier in weight, but standard sewing thread will work well. You may also want to make your stitches a little longer, maybe a 3.5–4.5 stitch length. And because topstitching is meant to show on the good side of the fabric, make sure that you don't run out of thread midway between your starting and stopping points – you want the stitch line to be continuous.

Serging (overlocking)

Serging is good for seams in stretchy fabrics like knitwear, because it still allows the fabric to stretch. These fabrics typically don't have clean edges when cut and may unravel, but when you feed your fabric through a serger it stitches by wrapping around the edge and at the same time also trims the fabric edge giving it a clean and durable finish. This has the dual function of giving the raw edges of a fabric a finished appearance, without folding a hem, and stabilizing the raw edge to prevent it fraying. Typically, it is used in this way on the underside of sewn items or in areas that are hidden from view but are still subject to wear.

Seams

Straight seam

Sometimes called simple seams, straight seams are used to join two pieces of fabric together with a seam and form one of the foundations of sewing. These seams are one of the most common ways to construct sewing projects, and when attaching patchwork pieces together. They don't technically have to be straight – they can follow the line of any fabric shape – but are typically created in the same way. The seam usually begins and ends with a short length of back stitching – which just means setting the machine to stitch backward for a few stitches before beginning the seam.

STEP 1 Place the fabric pieces to be joined on top of each other, right sides together, with both raw edges aligned. Pin in place.

STEP 2 Arrange one end so the needle will begin stitching a short distance along the seam, then back stitch to the start of the seam. Sew a line of straight stitches with a ⅜in (1cm) seam allowance along the entire length and finish with another short length of back stitching.

STEP 3 Open out and press the seam allowances flat – sometimes given as "press the seam flat" in patterns. Alternatively, you may be instructed to press both seam allowances to one side.

French seam

The French seam is another way of joining fabric together but concealing the raw edges. It results in a nice seam with a delicate appearance that has no visible stitch lines and no need for serging. Unlike a flat felled seam, which is flat on both sides, the French seam is flat on the right side with a visible fold on the back, which makes it a better seam for lightweight or translucent fabrics.

STEP 1 Place the two pieces of fabric wrong sides together – so with right sides out – and the edges to be joined neatly aligned. Sew with a seam allowance of ½in (1.25cm). When finished, trim the seam allowance back to ¼in (0.6cm) along the entire length.

STEP 2 Press the seam allowance to one side with an iron so that it is nice and flat. Next, fold the fabric along the stitch line so that right sides are now facing each other and press along the edge.

STEP 3 Stitch using a ½in (1.25cm) seam allowance, which will neatly encase the raw edges. Press the seam flat.

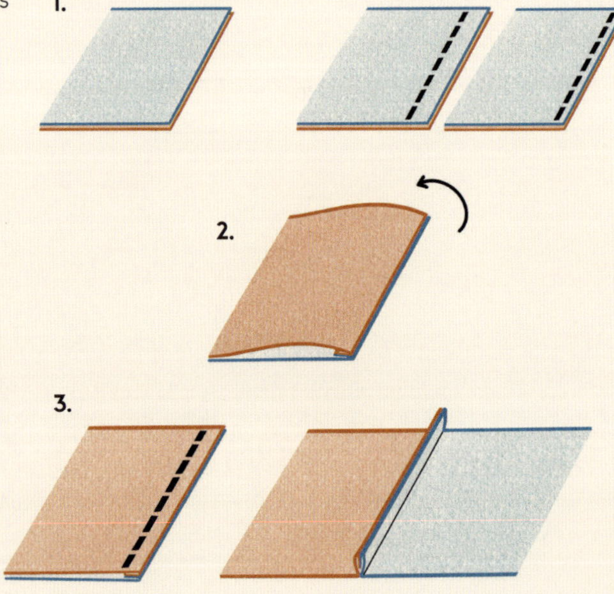

Flat felled seam

This is used for joining fabric pieces together where both sides of the fabric need to be finished with no raw edges or serging. The seam allowance on one of the pieces of fabric is longer than that of the other so that when it is folded over twice, and stitched down each time, the result is a strong, neat seam where all raw edges are hidden within the flat folds.

STEP 1 Place the two pieces of fabric wrong sides together – so with right sides out – and aligned along the edge where the seam is to be sewn. Then slide the top fabric back by ⅜in (1cm) away from the edge of the fabric beneath. The lower edge will now extend beyond the upper. Make sure the difference is even all the way down the edge. Feel free to pin the pieces in place before sewing.

STEP 2 Sew the two pieces together about ⅜in (1cm) stitch from the edge of the top piece of fabric.

STEP 3 Fold the longer bottom edge up and over the edge of the top piece. Pin in place if you like, making sure to keep the fold tight. The raw edge of the top piece is now hidden inside a fold.

STEP 4 Open up your fabric with both right sides still facing up. Fold the seam flat to one side so that both raw edges are now hidden within folds. Pin in place.

STEP 5 Lastly, stitch the fold down, close to the folded edge, along its entire length.

1.

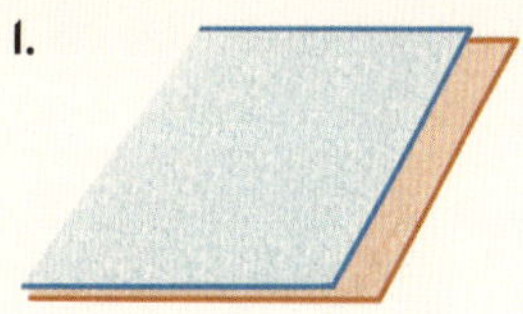

2.

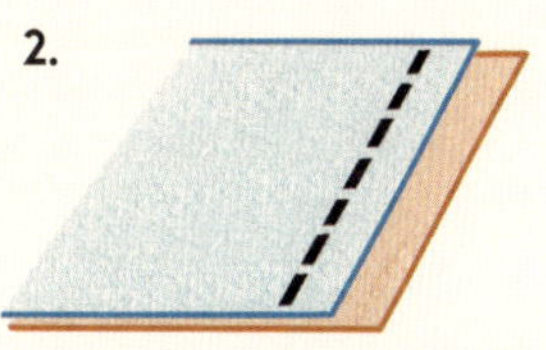

3.

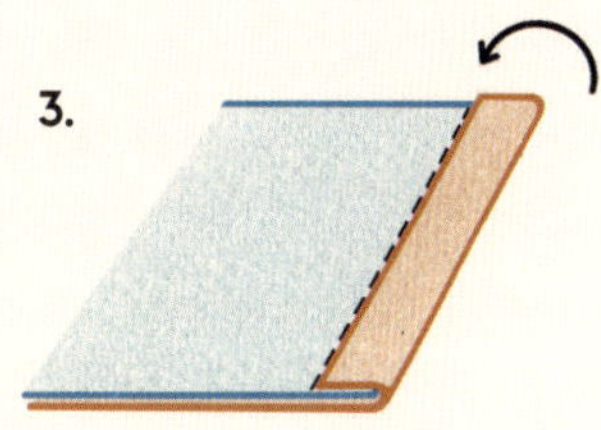

4.

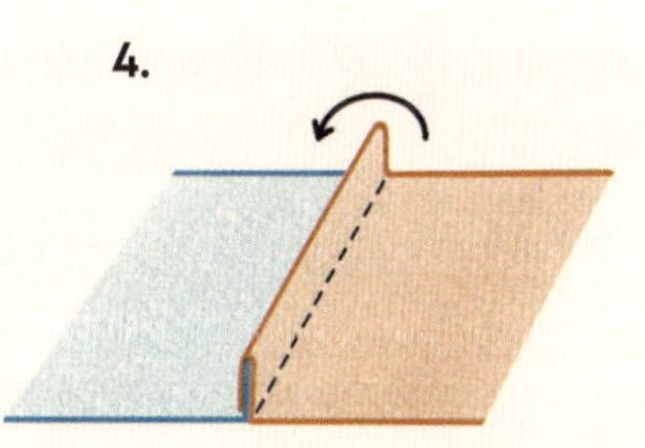

5.

Finishing edges

Hemming

A process of folding and sewing fabric edges, hiding the raw edge within the fold, to make a clean finished edge. There are a number of different types of hem, which can be either hand sewn or machine sewn. Some hems are more suitable for different fabrics than others. I typically use folded or turned hems, which are great for creating finished edges in clothing or home goods such as napkins or tablecloths. They can vary in appearance depending on choices such as depth, thread color, and by which stitch you choose. They can be narrow or wide with stitches that are prominent or hidden.

Start by folding the raw edge over on the wrong side of the fabric, then once more so the edge is hidden within the folds. Press the folds flat either by hand or with an iron, making sure to keep them as even as possible, and pin in place.

If hand sewing, the edge can be sewn in place with a variety of stitches such as a ladder/blind, catch, or whip stitch. Sew the hem down from the back, sewing close to the edge according to the chosen stitch. If machine sewing, stitch along the upper folded edge from the wrong side of the fabric, close to the edge, back stitching at the start and finish.

If your hem needs to turn a corner, square corners can be done very simply. First, complete the above steps on two sides opposite to each other on the item that you are hemming. Then complete the last two sides in the same way, folding the raw sides over twice, as well as each corner. Finish by sewing along the entire edge.

Pinked seam allowance

This refers to a type of finish on the raw edges of seam allowances whereby pinking shears, which are scissors with zigzag blades, cut a length of little diagonal zigzags along the fabric edge, resulting in less fraying as the fabric is worn. However, it usually only reduces fraying. To strengthen a pinked seam further, cut your pinked seams about a ¼in (0.6cm) from the edge and then add a row of straight stitches right next to the pinked edge.

Clipping and grading

When clipping curves you cut small triangular pieces of fabric from the seam allowances around the curves after sewing. Snipping away and removing some of the bulk lets the seam allowances curve more easily on the wrong side, so from the right side the curved edge appears smoother. This is also important when turning curved items right side out, where the clipping will not only improve the appearance, but also remove bulk between layers or in tight spaces. When clipping, use snips and be mindful not to damage the seam by cutting too much away or cutting into the stitching.

Grading is another technique to remove bulk, but where the two seam allowances are trimmed to different widths. Grading can be used on curved seams to reduce bulk and impart a smooth appearance, but can also be used on straight seams when pressing seams with too much bulk, or when seams have several layers of fabric.

Binding

Binding is a way to finish the raw edges of fabric constructions that consist of multiple layers of fabric, sometimes with an intermediary material such as batting (wadding), as in quilts. Binding can come in many forms, but typically it is a strip of fabric of any length that is wrapped around the raw edge and sewn in place giving a neat, finished appearance. Some edge bindings only need to be short sections consisting of single pieces of fabric, while for others you will need to join fabric strips to create a continuous strip the length you need. You may also have to contend with corners and ways to finish the ends.

Often binding is referred to as bias strip or tape, because the binding can be a strip of fabric cut on the bias (diagonally). There are aesthetic reasons for this, but mostly it is because fabric cut on the bias can be wrapped around corners continuously and neatly. However, cutting fabric diagonally can use a lot of fabric, which makes it difficult for me to balance my need to be economical with materials. So, more often than not, I tend to stick with straight cut binding strips when I am not dealing with curves.

There are two ways that I often use to sew on binding strips. Method one entails directly sewing the strip onto one side of the fabric before wrapping it around the edge and finishing. In method two the strip is pre-folded and placed over the raw edge, then sewn into place on both sides.

Binding an edge method one

STEP 1 Cut a fabric strip to your desired length, and about 2in (5cm) wide. If necessary, join multiple pieces together with simple seams, typically sewn on a bias.

STEP 2 Place the binding right sides together onto the fabric, aligning the raw edges of the binding and fabric. Pin in place about every 6in (15cm). Before beginning to sew, fold over the start of the strip by about ⅜in (1cm) – this will prevent a frayed edge.

STEP 3 Sew the binding in place with a ½in (1.25cm) seam allowance. At the other end, fold over the end by about ⅜in (1cm) again.

STEP 4 Now take the binding strip and wrap it around the edge. On the other side, fold under the raw edge and pin it down. Ladder stitch (see Ladder Stitch on page 31) the folded edge of the binding down.

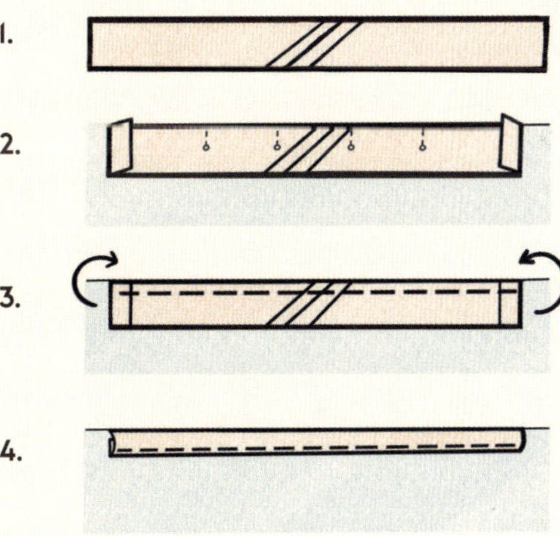

Binding an edge method two

STEP 1 Cut a fabric strip to your desired length, and about 2in (5cm) wide. Join multiple pieces together with simple straight seams if necessary.

STEP 2 Create a fold down the center by folding the binding strip in half lengthwise for the entire length with right sides facing out. Press the fold with an iron.

STEP 3 Fold the edges on both sides of the strip over towards the center fold, again with right sides facing out.

STEP 4 Slide the folded binding strip over all the raw edges of the fabric. Sew each edge to the fabric on both sides of the binding using a ladder stitch (see Ladder Stitch on page 31).

Tip

- Try using a bias tape folder and an iron to make the three folds in one simple action. Simply feed the strip in one end and pull through, ironing it flat as it comes out. Bias tape folders come in a variety of sizes

Binding all around with a straight corner

STEP 1 Make your binding strip as on page 23, about 2in (5cm) wide and long enough to go along one side of the item with an additional ¾in (2cm) to spare. Join as many individual pieces as necessary with simple straight seams.

STEP 2 Before beginning to sew, fold over both ends of the strip by about ⅜in (1cm) making sure that the now folded strip starts and stops right at both corners – this will prevent a frayed edge. Place the binding right sides together onto the fabric with raw edges aligned. Pin in place.

STEP 3 Sew the binding in place with a ½in (1.25cm) seam allowance. Now take the binding strip and wrap it around the edge. On the other side, fold under the raw edge and pin it down. Stitch the folded edge of the binding down with a ladder stitch (see Ladder Stitch on page 31).

STEP 4 Now that the binding on one side is complete, turn to the opposite side and repeat the process, making a strip long enough for the entire length plus an additional ⅜in (1cm) folded on both ends.

STEP 5 Next, turn to one of the unfinished sides and make a strip long enough for the entire length plus an additional ⅜in (1cm) left unfolded on both ends.

STEP 6 Sew in place as above, but start and finish sewing ⅜in (1cm) from the edges on both ends, and leave the extra fabric extending beyond the edge.

STEP 7 Now take the binding strip and wrap it around the edge. On the other side, fold under the raw edge and pin it down. Stitch the folded edge of the binding down with a blind stitch, again leaving ⅜in (1cm) unsewn at the beginning and end.

STEP 8 Finish the corners by folding the extra fabric under at each end and sew in place along the ends and bottom edges using a blind stitch.

Binding all around with mitered corner

STEP 1 Make your binding strip as on page 23, about 2in (5cm) wide and long enough to go all around the item with extra to spare. Join as many individual pieces as necessary with simple straight seams. Begin binding in the middle of one side, as in method one (see page 23), steps 2 and 3. Begin sewing just past the folded end so you can tuck the final end under it.

STEP 2 To make a mitered corner, stop sewing ½in (1.25cm) before you reach the corner and fold the binding strip down at a 90-degree angle, so that the edge of the binding strip is aligned with the edge of the next side. You have created a neat 45-degree fold right at the corner.

STEP 3 Fold the 45-degree corner up to the previously sewn edge, and continue sewing down the next side from the point you left off. Repeat at each corner and sew until you return to the point you started from. Overlap the end under the folded end at the start.

STEP 4 Now the sewing is complete on one side, fold the binding strip over to the other side on all four edges. Working on the other side now, fold the edge of the binding strip over by about ½in (1.25cm) so that the raw edges are tucked under, and pin the folded edges down. To create the corners on the back, fold down one side then the next to create a 45-degree mitered corner.

STEP 5 With the entire perimeter neatly folded and in place, sew the fold down with a ladder stitch (see Ladder Stitch on page 31).

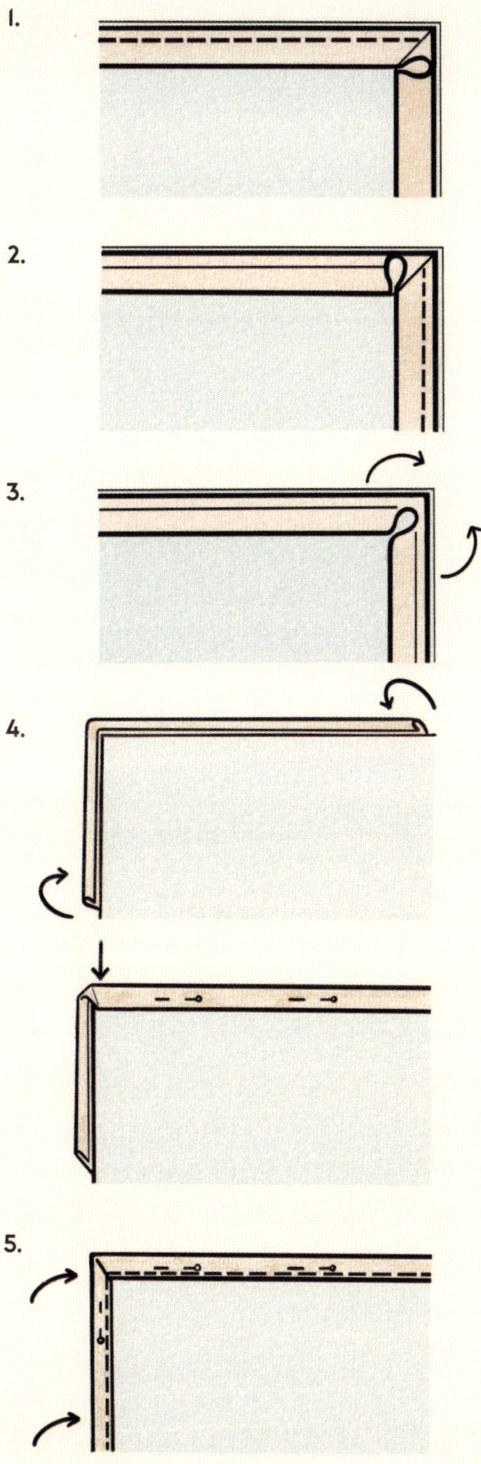

Construction techniques

Sewing gathers

While gathers involve sewing fabric to bunch it up, such as in clothing fitted around the waist, ruffles are gathers that are not specifically functional, but rather decorative in nature. I like adding ruffles to items such as pillows to create trims around their edges that add a sense of whimsy and fun. They can either be thin and minimal or wide and dramatic and give you all sorts of opportunities to add color, pattern, or texture to otherwise simple items. In all cases, the construction remains the same.

STEP 1 Cut strips of fabric – generally cutting along the grain of the fabric works best. And while ruffles can be made showing a right and wrong side, I prefer ones that are good on both sides. This means the width of the strips should be double your desired ruffle width plus two seam allowance of ½in (1.25cm) each. The length can vary depending on how tightly ruffled you want your item to be, but I find a good estimate to be about 1.5 x the total finished length of all combined sides of the item that you want to ruffle. If need be, sew shorter pieces of fabric together to make up the total length.

STEP 2 Place the two short ends together, right sides facing and aligned, and sew the ends together using a ⅜in (1cm) seam allowance to make the strip into a loop.

STEP 3 Fold the fabric over wrong sides together lengthwise so that the good sides are facing out. Press the fold and seams flat.

STEP 4 Fold the ruffle trim in half, and place a pin to mark each fold, then fold each side in half again the other way and place two more pins to mark the additional folds. This will give four equidistant points on the entire loop.

STEP 5 If using a sewing machine, set the stitch setting for a fairly long stitch, almost like a basting (tacking) stitch, and sew a line of straight stitches along the raw edge with about a ¼in (0.6cm) seam allowance. Start each line of stitches at one of the pins and end it at the next pin, leaving lengths of thread at each point where you start and stop with no back stitching. You will have completed a seam along the entire length of the ruffle trim but in four separate sections. For safety on longer edges, repeat to make a second line of stitching in the same way.

STEP 6 Now, fold the base item in half on all four sides and mark the midpoints with a water-soluble marker. With the base item right side facing up, place the ruffle trim on top, with the raw edges facing out and aligned with the raw edge of the base item. Secure the four pins on the ruffle trim to the four midpoints of the base item. This will ensure that the ruffle trim is evenly distributed (the ruffle will extend beyond the corners).

STEP 7 Gently, but firmly, pull one of the loose ends of thread with one hand, while ruffling the fabric along the thread with the other, to create even ruffles along one quarter of the base cloth – making sure not to pull the thread out on either end. If you have two lines of stitching you can knot the threads together to prevent them being pulled out. It may take some coaxing, but working in small sections, adjusting the folds and pinning them down as you go will help. Work from one quarter to the next in a similar way until the entire trim is ruffled and fits with the raw edge of the base item.

STEP 8 The last step is to place the other half of the base item fabric back on top (with zipper added accordingly and pulled slightly open), with all edges aligned and right side facing down (the ruffles will still be facing in at this point so hidden between the layers). Sew along all for sides with a ⅜in (1cm) seam allowance, followed by serging of all four sides. Turn right sides out through the zipper.

Sewing a zipper

There are a number of ways to sew a zipper for small projects such as pillows. A pillow zipper has different requirements to those for bags or clothing in that it is not meant to be used often as a means of closure. Rather, it is simply used to contain the pillow insert and otherwise not be seen. This method is perfect because it creates a small flap which hides the zipper from view.

STEP 1 Cut the pieces of fabric that will hold the zipper and serge the two edges where the zipper will be sewn.

STEP 2 Place the two fabric pieces right sides together, with the two serged edges aligned. Sew together for about 2in (5cm) only from each corner, with a seam allowance of ⅝in (1.5cm), leaving a large unsewn gap in the middle for the zipper. Press the edges of the seam over to give the unsewn gap neat and clean edges.

STEP 3 If you can, use a zipper foot so you can sew very close to the zipper teeth. Open out the two pieces of fabric with right sides facing up and place the zipper right side up underneath the unsewn gap. Align the zipper slightly off center so that side A will cover the teeth of the zipper completely. Pin in place.

STEP 4 Place the piece fabric side up in your machine, with side A towards the back. Start by sewing across the zipper at one end, then sew along the folded edge of side B very close to the zipper teeth. Continue sewing across the opposite end of the zipper and then finally along side A, this time sewing about ½in (1.2cm) from the folded edge. This will result in a flap on side A that covers the zipper from view.

STEP 5 If you are making a pillow, fold it along the zipper so it is right sides together and the remaining three sides are neatly aligned. Open the zipper slightly (it will be more difficult to open it from the wrong side when the other sides are all sewn). Pin around the perimeter and sew around all three remaining sides using ⅜in (1cm) seam allowance. Before turning right side out, serge the remaining edges and trim any loose threads. Turn right side out and press the edges.

Sewing a gusset

A gusset can mean several different things depending on what you are making, but commonly gussets refer to triangular pieces of fabric added to or created within an item to add more room or volume, without which it would otherwise be flat. They allow objects such as clothing or bags to expand and have more shape when used. Adding gussets affects their appearance but improves their functionality. Side gussets are the simplest resulting in a flat, square bottom. For the Lunch Bag on page 82 I added a simple accordion fold gusset to create depth along the side and bottom.

Accordion gusset

STEP 1 Create an accordion fold by first folding the fabric in half, right sides together, to create a line at the midpoint. Press flat. Fold one side over by 2¼in (5.75cm) from the midpoint and press flat.

STEP 2 Next, turn the fabric over and fold the top half over the previous two folds, 2¼in (5.75cm) from the midpoint, ensuring all four sides and folds are evenly aligned. Press flat.

STEP 3 Sew along the left and right sides using a ⅜in (1cm) seam allowance – at this point if you want the seam to be finished you can use a French seam (see French Seam on page 21).

Flat bottom / side gusset

STEP 1 Cut out a front and back panel and place one on top of the other with right sides together and all edges aligned.

STEP 2 Using a clear quilter's ruler and a pencil, measure and draw a square in the two bottom corners, with sides parallel with the fabric edges. Remember, the gusset width will be twice the size of the square you draw. Cut the squares out to create the gusset, being mindful not to clip beyond the drawn lines.

STEP 3 Sew the two sides and bottom of the panels together with a ⅜in (1cm) seam allowance and double stitching the start and finish points, leaving the top edge and corner squares unsewn.

STEP 4 Now fold to place one side seam over the bottom seam, making sure that all sides of the fabric are neat and flat and the sewn seams are also aligned and flat. This will pull the two unsewn edges of the square to align with each other in a straight line. Pin in place.

STEP 5 Sew straight across the gusset with a ⅜in (1cm) seam allowance, double stitching at start and end points.

STEP 6 Repeat steps 4 and 5 to sew the gusset seam on the other corner.

STEP 7 Turn right sides out.

Hand sewing

As with most sewing techniques there are two methods to hand sewing – stabbing in and out of the fabric to make each individual stitch, or sewing by loading the needle with several stitches at a time. Loading the needle allows you to work faster than working one stitch at a time and helps with consistency.

Running / straight stitch

A running stitch is one of the most common stitches used in all types of hand sewing, mending, and embroidery. It's equal to a sewing machine standard straight stitch. In appearance it resembles a continuous line of stitches separated by small gaps. The individual stitch length is determined by you, as is the length of the spaces between, but whatever you choose, they should be consistent and even across the entire length.

STEP 1 Thread your needle and tie a knot at the end (see Knots on page 34), then pull the needle through the fabric from underneath until the knot hits the fabric.

STEP 2 Next "load" the stitches onto your needle, about three at a time depending on the length of the needle, by pushing the needle under and over through the fabric. I usually try to keep the distance between stitches equal to the length of the actual stitches, but you may prefer a different spacing.

STEP 3 Pull the needle and thread through to finish the stitches, then repeat as many times as needed and finish underneath with a quilter's knot (see Knots on page 34).

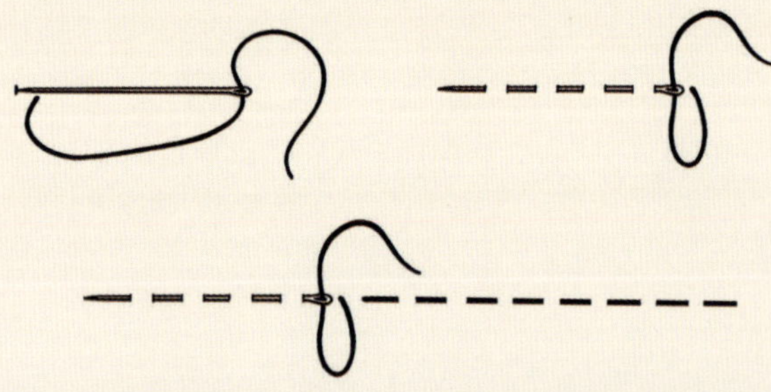

Basting (tacking) stitch

This is a temporary stitch used to hold pieces of fabric in place prior to permanent stitching and is sometimes used as a replacement for pins. In many ways it is similar to straight running stitches but with larger individual stitches and with longer spaces between. To create a basting stitch, follow the instructions for a running stitch opposite, but load your needle with fewer, longer stitches. Spread as many stitches as you need over an area in order to join the layers of fabric and keep them rather loose so that they are easy to snip and remove afterwards. It's best to use a thread that contrasts with the fabric so the stitches are easy to see when you come to remove them.

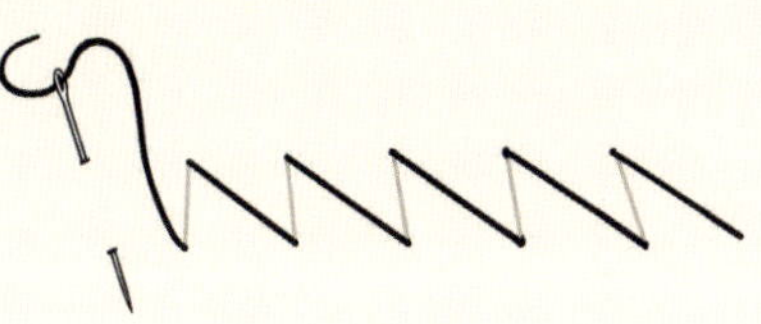

Whip stitch

A whip stitch is similar in essence to a running stitch because it's a continuous line of stitches with visible spaces between each stitch. However, rather than as a series of dashes in a single direction, these are stitched on an angle to the direction of the stitch line – or even perpendicular to it. While whip stitches can be used to create an edge, more often they are used along the edges of fabric such as where a layer of fabric is sewn onto another one, where two pieces of fabric are joined together, or where smaller pieces of fabric are sewn onto larger pieces such as in appliqué.

STEP 1 Position one fabric on the other and pin in place. Start your whip stitch underneath by bringing the needle up through the base fabric right next to the edge of the fabric you wish to join. Make a stitch over the edge, at a length and angle of your choice, and then down into both pieces of fabric.

STEP 2 With the needle now underneath again, bring it up through the base cloth next to the previous stitch, again at a distance of your choice.

STEP 3 Again, bring the needle and thread over the edge and back into both layers of fabric, keeping the distance and angles of each stitch consistent. Repeat until the edge is complete and both fabrics are sewn together. The edges of the fabric could be rolled under to form a neat edge first or left raw.

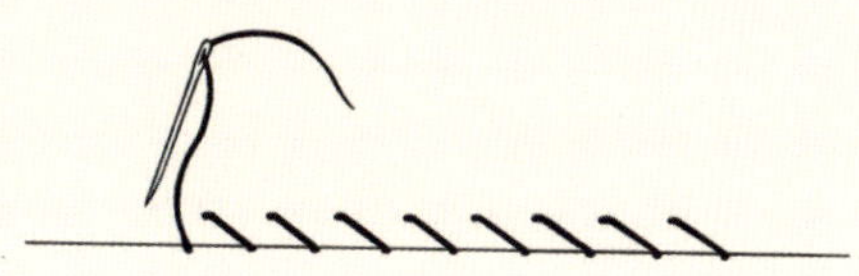

Back stitch

This stitch is especially important for creating imagery and patterns in embroidery but also when you want your sewing to have the graphic quality of a solid line. Unlike running stitches, it appears as a continuous line with little or no space in between the stitches, which is achieved by alternating between a forward, and then backward direction.

STEP 1 Thread your needle and tie a knot at the end (see Knots on page 34) before bringing your needle up through the fabric from underneath to the front until your knot hits the underside of the fabric. Make one stitch in a forward direction.

STEP 2 With the needle now underneath, bring it back through to the top one equally spaced stitch ahead of the previous stitch.

STEP 3 Next, go backwards and insert the needle down at the end of the previous stitch, making the stitch line appear unbroken.

STEP 4 With the needle underneath again, move forward one more stitch beyond the last one and then back on top to meet the previous stitch. A simple way to remember, in terms of spacing, is two spaces forward underneath, and one space back on top.

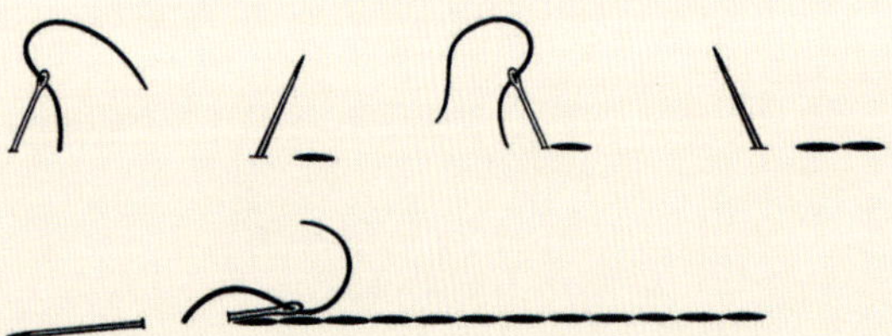

Blanket stitch

An expressive stitch that is typically used along the (sometimes raw) edges of fabric to create a finished edge, but is also considered decorative because it is visible from both sides and is often sewn in a contrasting color. Blanket stitches can also emphasize the edges of openings or can be used as a decorative element on their own as a surface stitch without any edge. Blanket stitches usually maintain consistent spacing, stitch lengths and entry/exit points for the needle, but feel free to establish your own spacing or alternate with different lengths.

STEP 1 When stitching along an edge the first stitch will be an anchor stitch. Start by tying a knot at the end of the thread (see Knots on page 34) and bring the needle up from the back through your fabric to the front – the distance from the edge is your choice, and this will be the stitch line where you will start each new stitch. Take the needle and thread and wrap it around the edge to the back, then up to the front again through the same hole that you started with to create a loop around the edge. To finish the anchor, slide your needle sideways under the loop you just made along the edge of the fabric in the opposite direction to where you will be working, and tighten.

STEP 2 For the first blanket stitch, from the front, insert the needle into the fabric at a point along the stitch line in the direction you will be working – the spacing is up to you. Now, go through to the back but before pulling through completely thread the needle up and underneath the loop from the previous stitch.

STEP 3 Pull the thread up to tighten so the stitch is straight and perpendicular to the edge.

STEP 4 Repeat these steps using the same spacing, going into the back, up to the edge and through the loop of the previous stitch.

STEP 5 When you have completed your last stitch, simply wrap your thread around the last loop at the top along the edge and tie a knot. Then take the needle back into the fabric and snip off excess thread.

edge

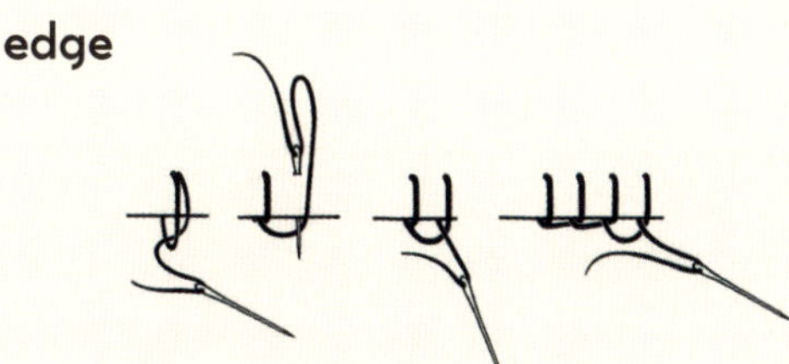

no edge

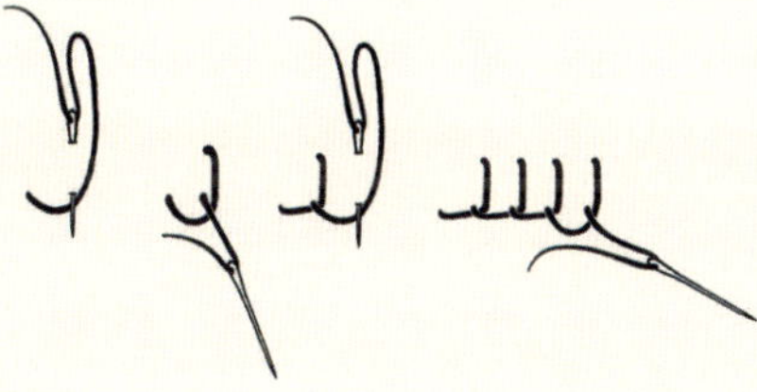

Ladder stitch

This stitch is also known as a slip or blind stitch and is used to join fabric together in such a way as to be as invisible as possible. It's perfect for closing seams where you have an opening after turning an item right side out, when you are sewing the binding onto an edge, or when simply joining the two edges of fabric together. In all cases at least one neatly folded edge is necessary to work through, so that the stitches can be hidden within the fold.

STEP 1 Fold both edges of the pieces of fabric to be joined to create a neat fold at the edge.

STEP 2 Thread your needle and tie a knot at the end (see Knots on page 34). At the starting point on one end, pull the needle up through the fold until the knot hits the fabric and is hidden inside the fold.

STEP 3 Hold the two folds together with one hand so that both edges are visible. Take the thread directly across from the knot to the opposite edge and slide the needle inside the fold for about ¼in (0.6cm) to create a small stitch underneath along the edge of the fold. Bring the needle back out and pull the thread tight. This will pull the two edges together.

STEP 4 Repeat, working back and forth, moving from one side straight across to the other, entering and exiting the fabric right on the edge of the folds and working laterally within the folds. When you have finished making ladder–like stitches across the entire gap, gently pull the two sides together to close.

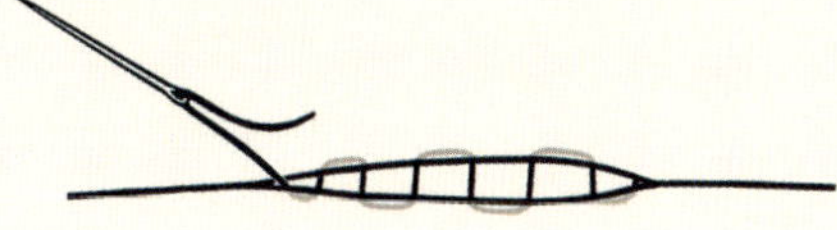

Catch stitch

Also known as herringbone stitch, this is another type of blind stitch that is used to create hems, or to join two pieces of fabric together where you want the thread to be minimally visible on the finished side. Because it consists of a row of X-shape stitches with a small back stitch at each point, it is perfect for stretchy fabric because the diagonals allow for movement.

STEP 1 With the wrong side of the fabric facing up, fold the edge of the fabric you will be working on to create a hem or seam with a single or double fold. If you are right-handed start on the left side, and on the right side if you are left-handed.

STEP 2 Thread your needle and tie a knot at the end (see Knots on page 34). Bring the needle through just below the fold and pull through until the knot is anchored inside the fold. Make a small stitch towards the left into the base cloth just above the fold to secure the thread.

STEP 3 Next bring the thread over the fold and down in a diagonal direction. Then, with your needle pointing backward to the direction that you are stitching, pick up a small stitch from the front folds of the hem only, making sure not to go through into the base cloth. This will keep the back stitch from being seen from the front.

STEP 4 Moving forward again, bring the thread up and over the fold in a diagonal direction. With your needle facing backwards again, pick up another small stitch in the base cloth above and close to the folded edge.

STEP 5 Repeat, alternating the "X" and small stitches until finished, then tie with a knot.

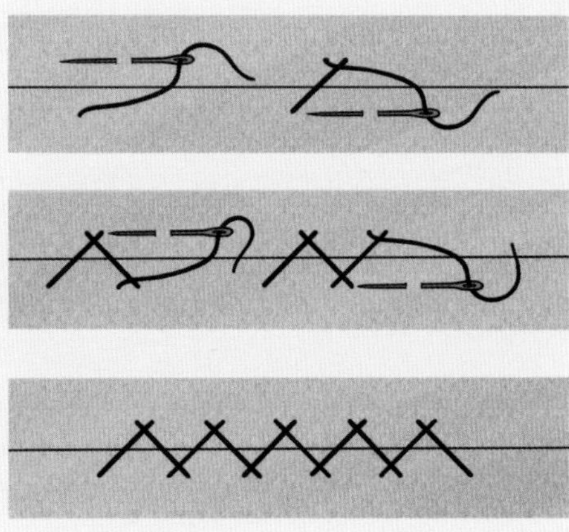

Sewing a button

Sewing buttons has many applications – as fasteners they can be paired with buttonholes, fabric loops, elastics, or left alone as decorative elements on the surface. And, of course, buttons come in many forms. But typical buttons with holes can be sewn in the following way.

STEP 1 Start with a very large knot on the end of your thread and pull the needle and thread up from the back of the cloth at the point that you want the button located. Slide the needle through one of the holes and bring the button down until it sits on the fabric.

STEP 2 Next, bring the needle back down through the diagonally opposite hole (if there are four holes) and into the fabric, then up through the hole you started with. Repeat this, coming up and back down, about four times. In some instances you will want to pull the threads nice and tight as you go for small buttons, but for larger buttons try to leave the thread a little loose so you can strengthen the threads as in step 5.

STEP 3 If your button only has two holes, you can now secure it by tying a knot at the back, but if your button has four holes then continue by moving to the empty holes and continue sewing, four times until your stitches result in an "X" on the front of the button.

STEP 4 For small buttons tightly sewn down just tie your thread off in a knot by taking the needle through the fabric to the back and then sliding it into the fabric until you form a loop. Pull the needle through the loop and pull to form a knot. Repeat a second time and snip the excess thread.

STEP 5 To strengthen larger buttons, and to leave a space between button and fabric for a fastener to sit, bring the needle down through one of the holes into the space between the button and the base fabric, then wind the thread tightly around the threads between the button and the fabric around four times or more. When done, take the needle and thread back into the fabric below and tie a knot.

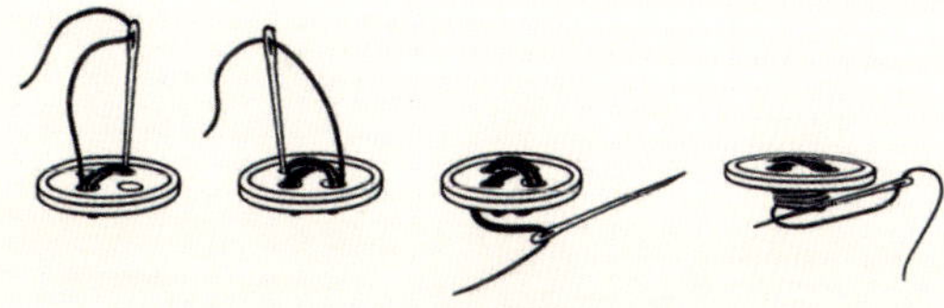

Knots

Most stitches start and finish with a knotted thread to secure the stitches and keep them from unraveling over time. Keeping your thread clean and trim is also visually appealing. Stitching usually starts and finishes on the wrong side to hide the end of the thread from view. Other times it is possible to leave knots on either side if you know that the stitch is in an area that will later be covered, such as with a binding, or if you start and finish stitches within a fold or between fabric, such as with a hem or seam, so the knots will be hidden in the layers.

Starting / quilter's knot

Cut a length of thread only as long as you need – estimate this based on the size of the project you are working on plus extra for a finishing knot. For larger projects I tend to cut a length that I am comfortable with – which for me is no longer than my arm's length – and then continue with additional lengths if I need to.

STEP 1 Feed the thread through the eye, and with two fingers pinch the tail of the thread against the needle, wrap the loose thread around and towards the tip of the needle several times – how many times will determine the size of the knot.

STEP 2 With one hand holding the needle tip and the other pinching the wrapped threads, slide the wrapped threads down towards the eye of the needle.

STEP 3 Continue to slide the wraps down over the eye until you reach the end of the thread.

STEP 4 At the end of the thread pull the wraps tight into a neat knot.

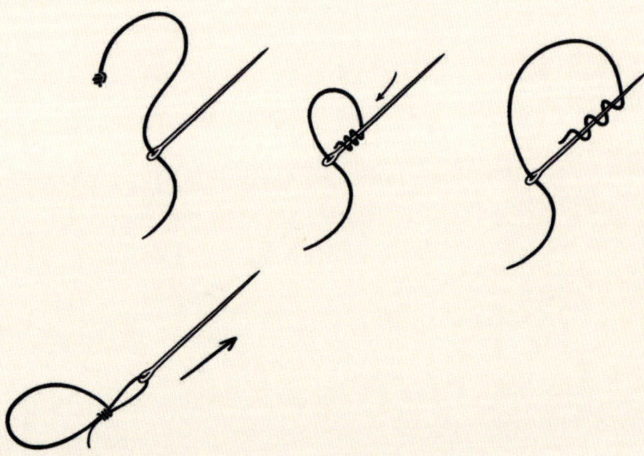

Finishing knot

This technique is best either on the back of a piece of fabric, along an edge that will be covered by binding, or within a fold.

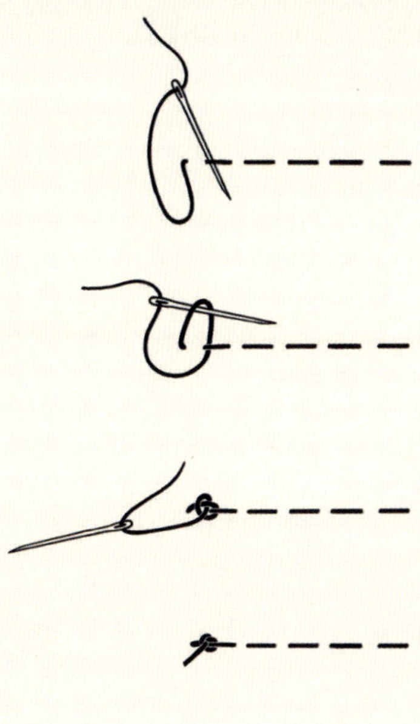

STEP 1 From below, bring the needle back and under the last stitch and pull the needle and thread until a loop forms.

STEP 2 Pass the needle through the loop.

STEP 3 Pull the knot forward until a knot is formed. Repeat If you want a larger knot.

STEP 4 Clip the thread to about ¼in (0.6cm).

STEP 5 Alternatively, if you are working with more than one layer of fabric, then take one additional stitch beyond where you want to stop, and tie a knot below both layers. Bring the needle back up through the same hole, remove the needle, and give the thread a tug, pulling the knot through the lower layer of fabric and into the space between. Carefully clip the loose thread left on top.

the projects

patchwork quilt

There are a lot of things about patchwork that I love, one being that it gives me reasons to save all my remnants, no matter what size, because you can work at any scale. It so happens that I had a pile of cotton fabrics, all with different prints and colors, that seemed perfect for a larger project like a quilt. Despite the size, there are a few ways to keep this project simple and surprisingly fast. For this one, I chose five different patterns, along with a solid, and quickly arranged a couple of rows in a random fashion by simply balancing lights, darks, and patterns. Then it was just a matter of repeating the rows as many times as you wish. The result has a nice organic quality that balances variety and movement with an overall structure that isn't too obvious. With that in mind, I also chose to forgo stitching by attaching the layers using the tie down method across the entire surface. It's relatively quick to do, and helps to emphasize a casual, handmade feel.

What you need

Approx. 3yd (2.75m) of fabric in a variety of prints and colors

Approx. 47 x 60in (119.5 x 152.5cm) of backing fabric

Approx. 47 x 60in (119.5 x 152.5cm) of low loft cotton batting (wadding)

Grid ruler

Rotary Cutter

Cutting mat

Scissors

Water-soluble marker

Chalk pencil (for darker fabrics)

Clips and safety pins

Sewing machine and sewing thread

Iron

Sashiko thread for ties

Sewing needle

Finished size

Approx. 47 x 60in (119.5 x 152.5cm)

Tips

- The number of patterns and amounts of each fabric is up to you. Don't worry about how many rectangles you cut at first – you'll need at least 101 for the size of quilt given but just cut a variety of what you have on hand, so you have a good selection to choose from.

- A total of 3yd (2.75m) will also give you enough fabric for the strips of binding (see Step 8).

Instructions

STEP 1

Cut 4 x 10in (10 x 25.5cm) rectangles from each fabric piece. On your worktable, start laying out pieces to create a row about 14 pieces wide. I created the first row by alternating groups of darks and lights with a free form variety of patterns. Once the first row is finished, create the second row above using the same grouping in different combinations. I made sure that the second row was slightly offset from the first like a brick pattern. Feel free to make some changes, such as making certain strips narrower or wider. Repeat these two rows, each above the other, three more times to make six rows in total. Lastly, repeat the first row one more time at the top so that the overall shape is a longer rectangle.

STEP 2

Now, sew the individual pieces together to create each row of 14. Start by placing the first two pieces right sides together with all edges aligned. Sew together along the long side using a ⅜in (1cm) seam allowance, backstitching as you start and stop. Next, repeat by joining the next piece to the previous pieces, until each row is finished. Press all the seams flat once the rows are sewn together.

STEP 3

With seven rows finished, start sewing the rows together. Place one row on top of the next, right sides together, aligned along the edge that is to be sewn. Sew along the edge with a ⅜in (1cm) seam allowance. Repeat until all rows are joined together. Press all the seams flat when finished. On a table, lay the patchwork flat and trim the two long sides if they are uneven.

STEP 4

Working on a large table, cut the batting and backing fabric slightly larger than the patchwork front. Place the backing fabric right side down and flatten. Next, place the batting on top of the backing, flattening and aligning, and finally the top patchwork front with right side up. Take time to smooth out and flatten all the layers and adjust them so that the top layer doesn't extend beyond the others. Place safety pins over the whole surface every 12in (30cm) or so to hold the three layers together.

STEP 5

Using a water-soluble marker or chalk, mark locations where the ties will go – I marked spots roughly 4in (10cm) apart from each other beginning 3½in (9cm) from the outside edges, with each row staggered, covering the entire quilt.

STEP 6

Thread a needle with a length of Sashiko thread with no knot at the end. Start tying along the edge of one of the short sides. From the front of the quilt, at each mark, go down with the needle to the back and then up ¼in (0.6cm) away. Pull the needle through and leave a 2in (5cm) tail on top. Cut the thread, leaving a 2in (5cm) end. Use the tails to make a square knot by creating a double loop and pulling it tight. Repeat this a second time and then trim the tails to about ¾in (2cm) long. Repeat this over the entire surface, making sure to continually smooth out the fabric before making each knot and that the thread goes through all three layers. If you need to, gently roll the quilt up as you go, keeping the roll a few knots away from where you are tying so the layers don't bunch up.

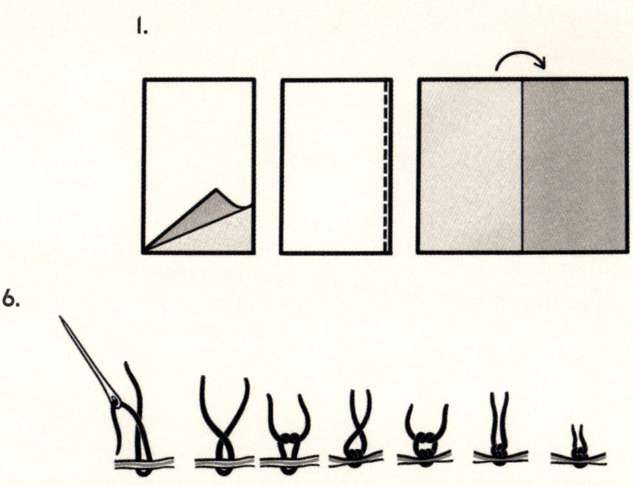

STEP 7

When all the ties are done, trim the layers all around the quilt so that all the edges are neatly aligned.

STEP 8

I used remnant fabric from the patchwork front for the binding so that the border has a patchwork look as well. Cut pieces in various patterns and random lengths into 1½in (4cm) wide strips and sew the short ends together in the same way as the patchwork pieces in previous steps to make a strip long enough to go around all four sides of the quilt with a bit extra (see Sewing Techniques: Binding All Around with Mitered Corner on page 25 for more detailed binding instructions).

STEP 9

Starting in the middle of one side, pin the binding strip on top, good sides facing the quilt front, with raw edges aligned. Sew with a seam allowance of ⅜in (1cm) all around the perimeter, making a miter at each corner. Once sewn on the front, flip the quilt over and fold the binding over to the back. Create a hem to hide the raw edge by folding the edge of the binding under. Pin in place and hand sew down using a ladder stitch (see Sewing Techniques: Ladder Stitch on page 31).

patchwork pillow

Patchwork is one of the most common, accessible, and enjoyable sewing techniques. In part this is because it is rooted in the age-old idea of embracing an economy of means and using what you have on hand – something that appeals to the utilitarian in me. But also because it so perfectly embodies the idea of making with fabric... cutting, combining, and sewing. Quite often I make patchwork that enjoys a certain organic and free-form quality, but in this case I wanted to make a cover for a pillow loosely based on the log cabin, where you start with a center piece and go around with strips of fabric. There is still room to combine large or small remnants with plenty of color, but visually it's a little quieter. Try making more than one, each with their own color combinations.

What you need

Approx. 7in (18cm) square of yellow fabric

3in (7.5cm) wide strips of the following:

- 10in (25.5cm) in each of pink and peach fabrics
- 11in (28cm) in each of red and light brown fabrics

4 x 60in (10 x 152cm) of dark yellow fabric

18 x 18in (46 x 46cm) of backing fabric

Grid ruler

Pencil

Scissors

Pins

Sewing machine

Sewing thread

Zipper foot (if you have one)

16in (40cm) zipper

18 x 18in (46 x 46cm) pillow insert

Finished size

18 x 18in (46 x 46cm)

Tip

- I used five different colors, plus the border colors. Step 1 shows the exact lengths that I used but when patching it is a good idea to cut the strips a little longer so you have some extra fabric to play with if necessary. You can also use your own color scheme according to what you have on hand.

Instructions

STEP 1

Start by cutting the center to 6½ x 6½in (16.5 x 16.5cm). For the surrounding 3in (7.5cm) strips cut the following:

- **Pink** – one 4¾in (12cm) and one 4½in (11.5cm) length
- **Peach** – one 2½in (6.5cm) and one 6½in (16.5cm) length
- **Red** – one 3½in (9cm) and one 7in (18cm) length
- **Light brown** – one 3in (7.5cm) square and one 7½in (19cm) length
- **Dark yellow** – two 11¾in (30cm) lengths and two 18in (46cm) lengths

STEP 2

Place the longer pink piece right sides together with the shorter peach piece, aligning one short end. Sew together with a ⅜in (1cm) seam allowance to make the longer strip 1, then press the seam open. Repeat with the longer peach piece and the shorter red piece to make strip 2, the longer red piece with the shorter light brown piece to make strip 3, and finally the shorter pink piece and the longer light brown piece to make strip 4. You can join the strips in any proportion you like – I find avoiding symmetry makes the composition more dynamic.

STEP 3

Next, lay strip 1 with right sides together on the center square with one edge of each aligned. Sew the two together with a ⅜in (1cm) seam allowance. Trim any extra fabric at either end of the strip so it's the same width as the square. Next rotate the square to sew on strip 2, arranging it so the peach forms an "L" shape at the corner. Add strips 3 and 4 in order, in the same way. Press the seams open and then press the piece after you finish sewing. This completes the "log cabin" section so you now need to add the border.

STEP 4

Next, patch the outer border around the center. Decide which side will be the top of the pillow and sew the two shorter dark yellow strips onto the left and right sides of the center patchwork in the same way as in step 3, again with a ⅜in (1cm) seam allowance. Trim any sides and press. Finish by sewing the remaining two long strips on the top and bottom sides of the patchwork. Press the entire piece and serge (overlock) the bottom edge.

STEP 5

Cut the fabric for the pillow back if necessary to match the pillow front and serge one edge – this will be the bottom edge.

2.

3.

6.

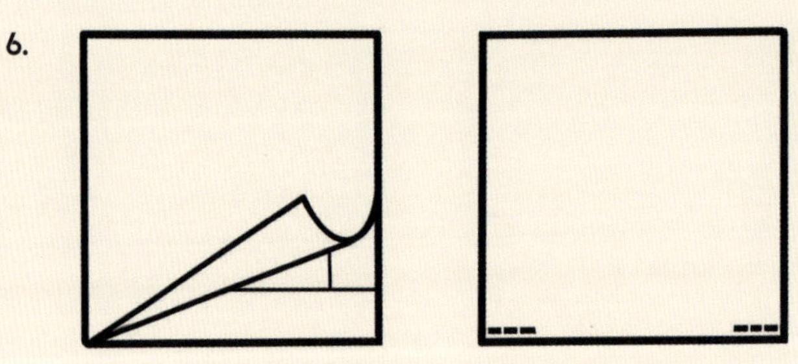

7.

8.

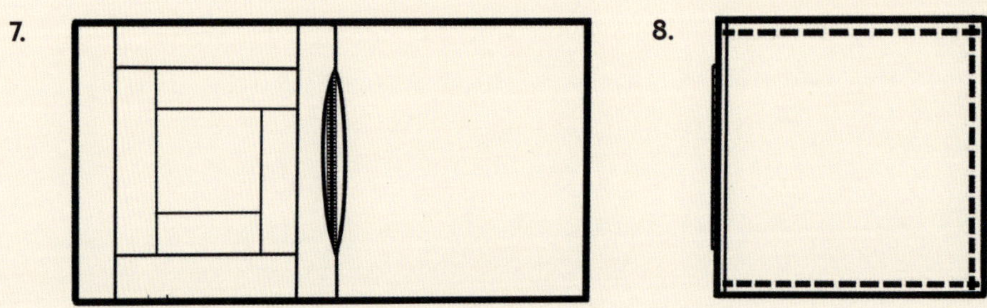

STEP 6

Pin the patchwork front and the back of the pillow right sides together and with the two serged sides aligned. Beginning about 2in (5cm) from the corner on the serged edge, sew with a ⅝in (1.5cm) seam allowance to the corner. Sew from 2in (5cm) along to the corner on the other side of the serged edge, leaving the center section of the serged edge open for the zipper. Press the edges of the seam over to give the unsewn gap neat and clean edges.

STEP 7

Using a zipper foot will allow you to sew very close to the zipper teeth. Open out the pillow with right sides facing up and place the zipper right side up underneath the unsewn gap. Align the zipper slightly off center so the patchwork side lies over the zipper teeth and pin in place. With the pillow cover right side up in your machine, start by sewing the zipper across one end, then sew along the folded edge of the pillow back very close to the zipper teeth. Continue sewing across the opposite end and then finally along the fold of the pillow front, this time sewing about ½in (1.2cm) from the zipper teeth. This will result in a flap on the pillow front that covers the zipper from view.

STEP 8

Fold the pillow along the zipper so right sides are together and pin around the perimeter. Sew around the three remaining sides with a ⅜in (1cm) seam allowance. Serge the edges and trim any loose threads. Turn the pillow right side out and press the edges. Lastly, add a pillow insert.

bowl covers

There was a time when tea towels were not the only textiles in the kitchen. All sorts of reusable items contributed to daily tasks, such as this simple and reusable bowl cover that can be used for covering leftovers, protecting fruit, or for keeping your dough warm. It is a great way to create a more eco kitchen by using less single-use plastic wrap and the cover can also be modified to suit your needs – an unwaxed cover allows oxygen to flow freely, while a waxed cover offers a better seal. I also make smaller ones that are good to go over jars. Use a lightweight fabric in a similar weight to quilting fabric or shirting. The amount you might need depends on the size of your bowls and how many you want to make, and if you want each bowl cover to be a different pattern you will need an assortment of fabrics. This project can be done on a sewing machine or sewn by hand.

What you need

Approx. ¼yd (23cm) of lightweight cotton fabric
1in (2.5cm) wide cotton twill tape (see step 2 for length needed)
¼in (0.6cm) wide elastic tape to fit circumference of bowl less 2in (5cm)
Ruler
Water soluble marker
Scissors
Pins
Sewing machine or hand sewing needle and thread
Bodkin or large safety pin to pull elastic through
Wax (optional)

Tips

- For several covers in various sizes, ¼yd (23cm) of a full width of fabric should be fine. It's a great way to use up old dish towels.

- Tape lengths for typically sized bowls are as follows:

  8in (20cm) diameter plus 2in (5cm) seam allowance: approx. 38in (96.5cm) length.

  9in (23cm) diameter plus 2in (5cm) seam allowance: approx. 42in (106.5cm) length.

  10in (25.5cm) diameter plus 2in (5cm) seam allowance: approx. 45in (114cm) length.

Finished size

To fit your bowl

Instructions

STEP 1

Cut the fabric into squares the width of the bowl diameter plus an additional 2in (5cm).

Place your fabric on a table right side down. Turn the bowl upside down and place it on the fabric, making sure to have an extra 1in (2.5cm) of fabric all around. Trace around the bowl using a water-soluble marker. Then, using a ruler, make a larger circle by adding an additional 2in (5cm) to the diameter (1in/2.5cm extra all around). Cut along the line of the larger circle.

STEP 2

Measure the length of the twill tape needed by placing it around the circumference of the larger circle plus an additional 2in (5cm) so you can turn the edge under. As an alternative, you can replace the twill with bias tape made from the same fabric as the bowl cover (see Sewing Techniques: Binding on page 23), cut to the same length as the twill tape and about 1½in (4cm) wide. I like using the twill tape because it has a finished edge and when I sew it down there is no bulk.

STEP 3

Start by folding the end of the tape over to the front by about 1in (2.5cm). Pin the twill tape around the raw edge of the fabric circle on the right side of the fabric. Sew all around using a ¼in (0.6cm) seam allowance and easing the tape into a curve. At the end of the seam, overlap the other end of the tape over the folded end. If you are sewing by hand, use a back stitch or closely spaced running stitches (see Techniques: Running Stitch on page 28). Now fold the twill tape right over so that it's now sitting on the wrong side of the fabric – the folded end at the start will now cover the other raw end. Sew a topstitch all along the unsewn edge, close to the edge, leaving a 2in (5cm) gap in the seam. If sewing by hand, use small, neat running stitches.

STEP 4

Cut the elastic tape to length by wrapping it around the top of the bowl but less 2in (5cm). Using a safety pin or bodkin feed the elastic through the casing formed by the twill tape until both ends come out of the opening. Sew the ends of the elastic tape together and finish sewing the gap in the twill tape. Now it's all ready to use.

STEP 5

To wax your own fabric, lay it out flat on top of a sheet or parchment to protect your worktable. Rub a beeswax bar over it or sprinkle pellets or shavings evenly across the surface then apply heat – a hair dryer or iron – to melt the wax. If you use an iron, also place a sheet of parchment on top of the fabric to protect your iron. Wax can be reapplied if you missed a spot. Allow to cool completely before using.

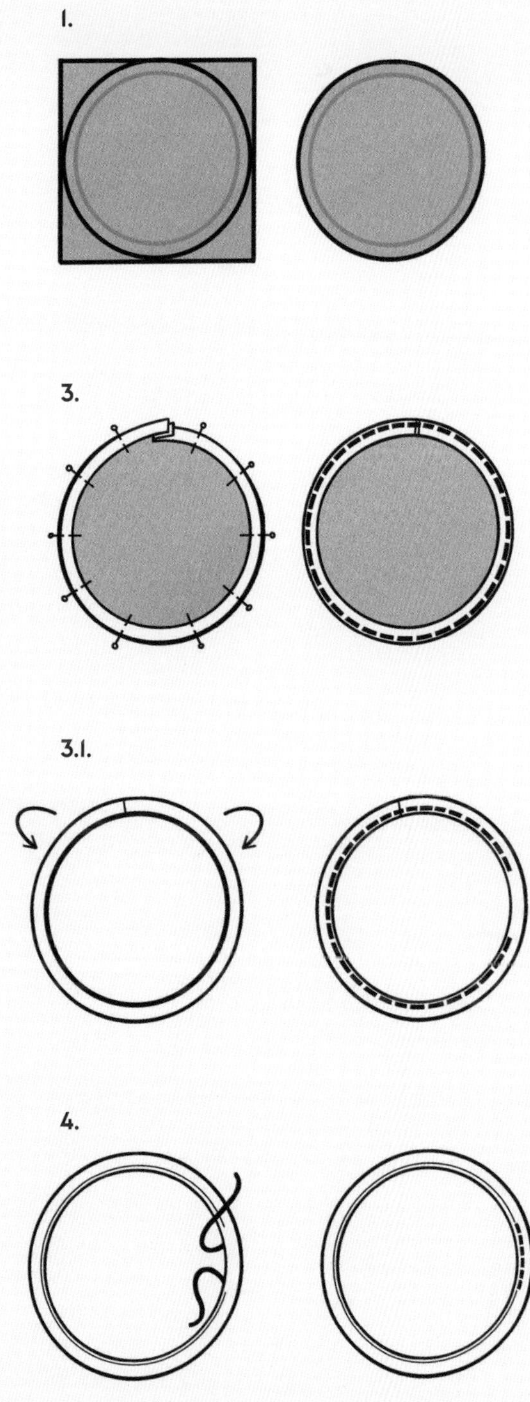

table runner

Sometimes we have to remind ourselves that table settings aren't just for mealtimes. A table with lovely textiles is always a great place to spend some time. This table runner has a nice natural feel using linen, with a repeat pattern stitched with Sashiko thread that gives it a subtle hand-made feel. With color, texture, and detail, it will add visual interest to the entire room. This project can be done without a sewing machine

What you need

Approx. 61 x 16½in (155 x 42cm) of medium weight fabric
Approx. 61 x 16½in (155 x 42cm) of cotton muslin (calico) fabric
Tape measure
Scissors
Sewing machine or hand sewing needle and thread
Grid ruler
Water-soluble marker
Pins or safety pins
Sashiko sewing needle
100yd (92m) of natural color Sashiko cotton thread
Snips

Finished size

15½ x 60in (39.5 x 152.5cm)

Tips

- I used a linen and cotton blend for my runner.
- You can also use cotton embroidery floss as an alternative to the Sashiko thread.

Instructions

STEP 1

Choose your fabric and color – I chose a dark yellow fabric because it goes well with the warmth of a wooden table, and I prefer the natural look and weight of linen. I also chose a natural color Sashiko thread so the stitching would be subtle with less contrast. Before starting, prepare all your fabrics by washing to remove any starch or sizing, and iron flat when dry.

STEP 2

Cut the two main fabrics to 16½ x 61in (42 x 155cm) if necessary and place them right sides together, with all four sides aligned. Sew all around the edge using ½in (1.25cm) seam allowance, leaving a 3in (7.5cm) unsewn opening midway on one of the long sides. Clip across the four corners to avoid bulk, then turn the runner right side out through the unsewn gap, making sure the corners are pushed out and square. Press the seams flat with an iron, making sure all the sides are straight with no fabric tucked inside along the seams. Hand sew the open gap closed with a ladder stitch (see Sewing Techniques: Ladder Stitch on page 31).

STEP 3

Using a grid ruler, measure a border 2½in (6.5cm) from the outside edge around all four sides and then use a water-soluble marker to mark a line. Using the water-soluble marker again, and starting at one end of the fabric, draw circles in various random sizes, making sure they are no larger than 6in (15cm) in diameter. Make the circles slightly irregular, or just half circles to fill in places along the border, but try not to overlap the shapes. I also added lines within each circle to divide it into segments and add more detail. After you finish drawing, use safety/straight pins to baste (tack) the two layers of fabric together across the surface to help stop the layers from shifting as you stitch.

STEP 4

Cut an arm's length of Sashiko thread and tie a knot at the end. Starting from the back, sew a running stitch (see Sewing Techniques: Running Stitch on page 28) around each circle design. Try to complete each circle and its division lines one at a time then tie off the thread on the back with a knot. This will minimize the amount of stringing thread from circle to circle on the backside and so will keep the back of the piece looking much neater. Try not to pull the stitches too tight to avoid puckering.

STEP 5

When the stitching is complete, use a spray bottle to spritz water over the surface to erase the drawn lines. Give the piece a press and it's ready to be used.

2.

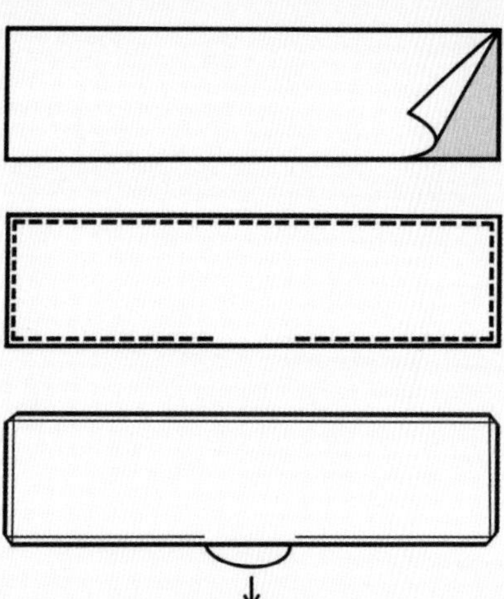

4.

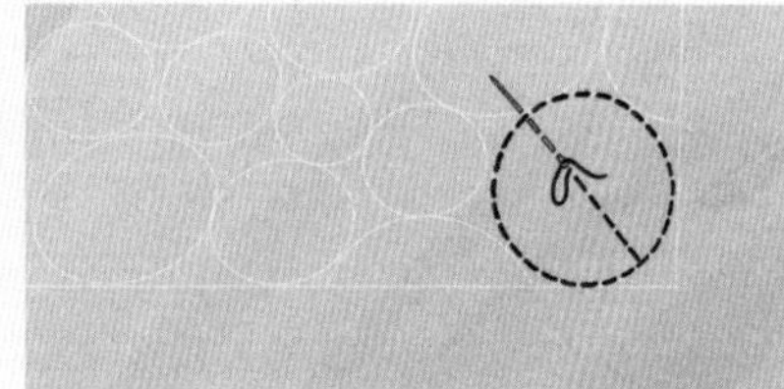

drawn thread tablecloth

Drawn thread is a centuries old technique that is related to lacework, quite often accompanied by embroidery, to create highly decorative and ornamental patterns on woven cloth. What separates drawn thread from other types of work on cloth is that patterns start not by adding something, but by removing: threads, either from the warp or weft, or sometimes both, are cut and pulled out to create open spaces in the weave. Patterns are then enhanced by stitches and details woven back into the remaining fabric, which when combined with the open spaces creates an impressive visual impact. This project references an age-old technique but is one that focuses on the basics. By simply removing a few threads and adding a hemming stitch, you will create a decorative border that will give your tablecloth a special design but in a clean and altogether modern way.

What you need

Linen fabric in a size for a tablecloth (see tip)
Tape measure
Scissors
Water-soluble marker
Grid ruler
Small snips
Tweezers (optional but helpful to pull thread from small areas)
Embroidery needle size 5
Top stitching thread, or size 12 Perle cotton thread

Finished size

54 x 54in (137 x 137cm)

Tips

- Using the width of the bolt as my guide, I cut a square piece of linen fabric sized 54 x 54in (137 x 137cm).

- Top stitching thread is a little heavier than sewing thread. I used an off white 12wt thread.

Instructions

STEP 1

Start by cutting your fabric to size. This is an important first step because it helps to have the fabric, with the selvage removed, cut along the grain of the weave so that all sides are neat and squared. If cutting along the grain is difficult, you can establish a straight edge by removing a few threads and then trimming with scissors.

STEP 2

Now measure and draw the areas of thread to be removed. Using a grid ruler, measure 1in (2.5cm) from the edge of the cloth and draw a line with a water-soluble marker along the entire length of every side of the cloth. Next measure ½in (1.25cm) in from the first line, and draw a second line, again the entire length of each side. Repeat to draw a third line at 1in (2.5cm) in from the second line and a final line ½in (1.25cm) in from the third line. These four lines indicate the areas where you will be working: the first line along the outside will mark the hem line, and the two zones that are ½in (1.25cm) wide will have threads removed.

STEP 3

The first areas of thread to be removed are at the four corners. For this design, it's important that the drawn threads (those to be removed) should not extend right to the edge of the fabric, so the 1in (2.5cm) edge remains solid to form a complete hem all the way around the tablecloth. If you pull the thread to the end of the cloth, it will make sewing the hem under more difficult with threads missing. In addition, in each corner the lines of drawn thread from adjacent sides meet, and there will be two open spaces at each corner (A, B) with no threads; to avoid leaving these spaces showing the ends of raw threads, the threads need to be cut with tails of about 1½in (4cm) long that can be threaded back into the weave (A), and similarly cut and folded back so they can eventually be hidden within the hem (B).

STEP 4

Referring to diagram 3 on page 63, snip the threads in two locations at each corner square. To do this, use a needle to separate and spread the threads, and pull them up out of the weave before carefully cutting the threads with some snips. Remember, you are only cutting either the warp or weft at each location. With a needle, feed the thread end back into the weave one at a time, clipping the ends if necessary, until all threads are neat and secure. Repeat this process at all four corners at location (A) only.

STEP 5

When the corners are complete, start to pull out the remaining thread from each side, being mindful not to snip any threads that are not meant to be removed. Carefully pulling the threads in sections of 6in (15cm) or so will make it easier and avoid puckering. Finish one side before moving to the next until all sides are done.

STEP 6

Prepare the edges for a hem on all four sides. On the wrong side fold the raw edge over about ⅜in (1cm) from the edge making sure to crease the fold. Then fold over once more making sure that the raw edge of the fabric is tucked under and the folded edge lines up to the bottom of the first section of drawn thread. Pin in place, and repeat on the remaining three sides, folding neatly at all four corners. Remember to tuck the ends of the loose threads from step 4 into the hem.

STEP 7

Lastly, secure the hem in place with a whip stitch (see Sewing Techniques: Whip Stitch on page 29) while at the same time stitching into the drawn thread. Thread a needle and tie a knot at the end. Starting at one corner, working from the wrong side, begin inside the fold at the corner on the wrong side, bring the needle through to the front, then take a small stitch and go back into the hem, before crossing diagonally again to go back into the base cloth. Repeat this until you get to the beginning of the drawn thread section.

STEP 8

At this point, coming up from the top of the hem on the back, use the tip of the needle to pick up the first six threads from the drawn thread section. Wrap the needle around the threads creating a little bundle, and pull the thread taut, but not enough to cause the fabric to pucker. Next make one whip stitch more, going from the front of the base cloth through to the edge of the hem. Repeat, picking up six threads underneath, wrapping around them, then make a whip stitch into the fabric as before. Continue until each side is complete.

2.

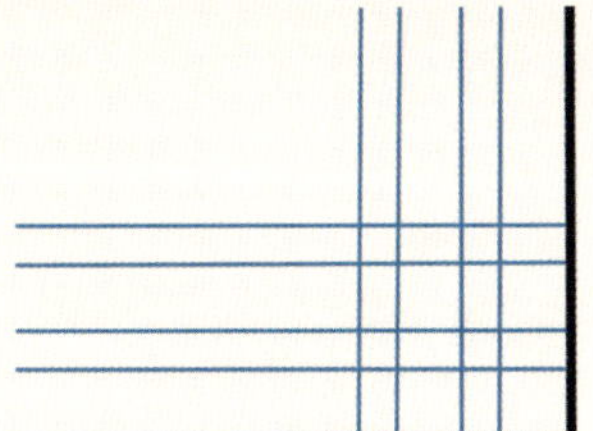

3.

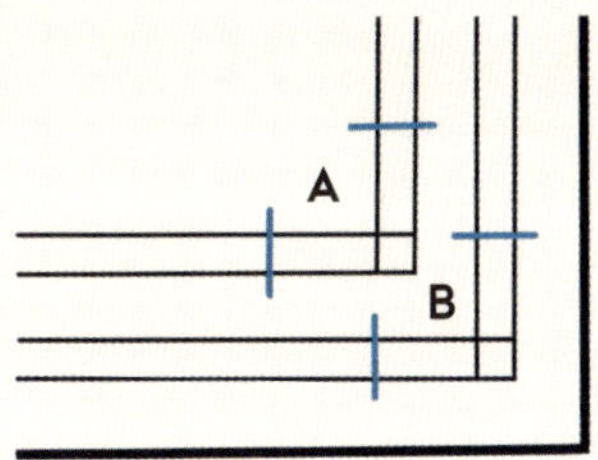

4.

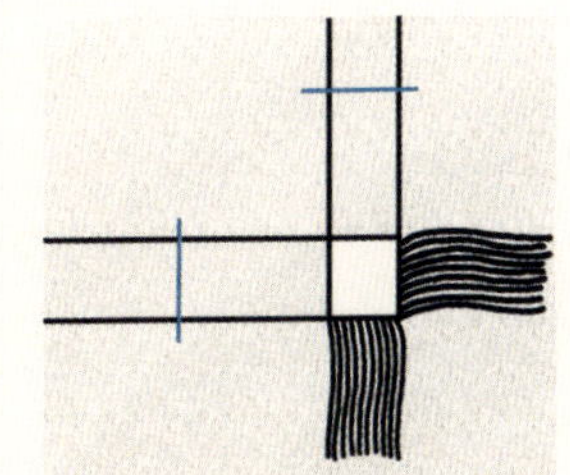

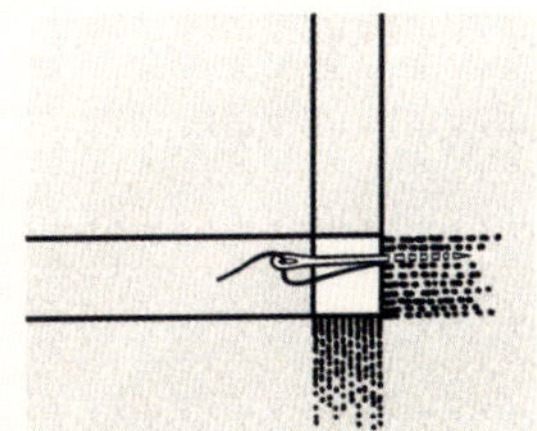

6.

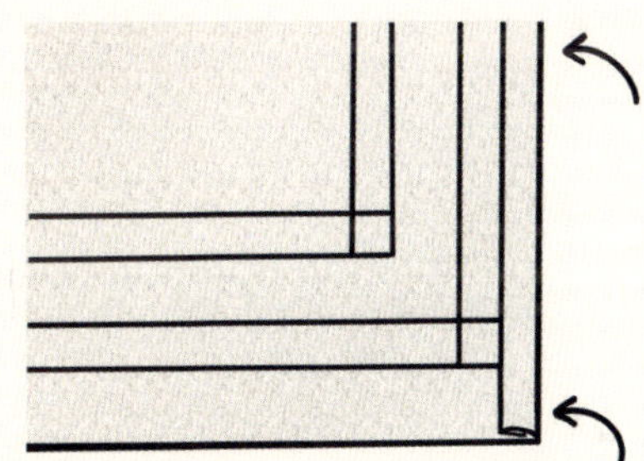

7.

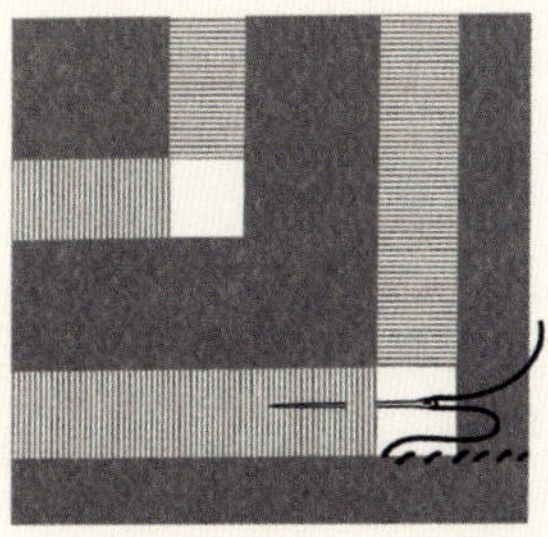

8.

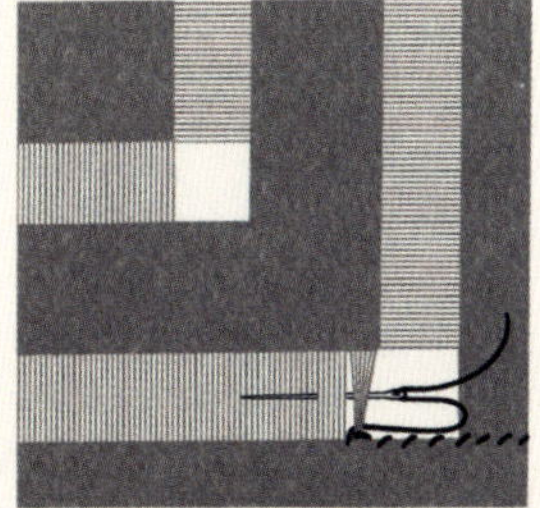

napkins with trim

Napkins are one of those items that elevate any occasion, and creating your own can really add a personal touch to your table. I used ric rac trim along the edges to add some graphic detail, color, and just a hint of whimsy. Ric rac can be used in various color combinations and there are many ways to sew the trim to the napkins – I chose to sew it to the back, just under the seam, to give the edge a minimal scalloped effect. You can use existing napkins or make your own, experimenting with different colors and textures. You can also use the same steps to create a tea towel, you just need to adjust the scale of your piece.

What you need

19 x 19in (48 x 48in) of lightweight fabric for each napkin
2¼yd (2m) of ¼in (0.6cm) wide ric rac trim in any color
Ruler
Water-soluble marker
Scissors
Pins
Sewing machine or sewing needle and thread

Finished size

18 x 18in (46 x 46cm)

Tips

- Various textures and weights of fabric will do; I prefer to use a lightweight fabric like a shirting weight.
- You can substitute a different trim for the ric rac.
- Multiply the amounts for one napkin by how many napkins you want to determine the total amount of fabric and ric rac you will need.
- You can also follow these instructions to create a tea towel, although I would suggest a slightly heavier fabric. You may also want to adjust the finished size to 18 x 24in (46 x 61cm). You could try different trim on the short side only rather than around the whole perimeter.

Instructions

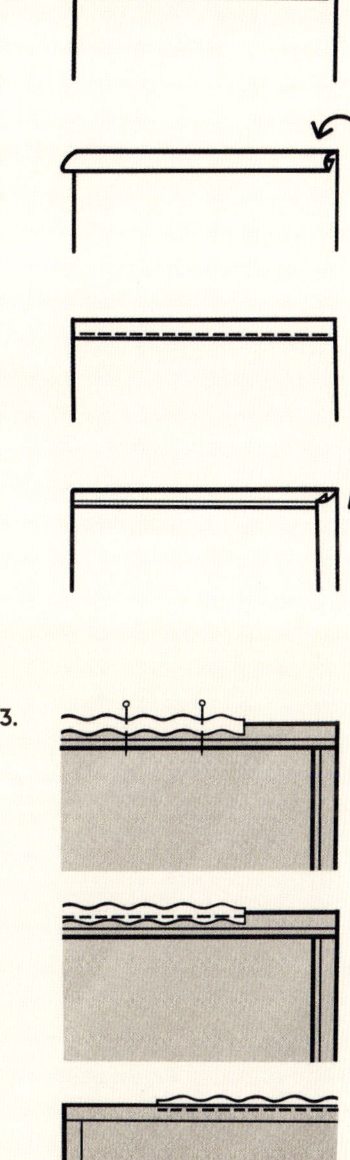

STEP 1

Draw 19 x 19in (48 x 48cm) squares onto your fabric with corners squared and making sure the lines run along the grain of the fabric. Cut out each piece.

STEP 2

Sew rolled hems all around each square by folding over the edge by ¼in (0.6cm) to the wrong side and then folding once more to tuck in the raw edge, then pin in place. Sew along close to the edge of the inside fold. Sew each corner with a neat fold (see Sewing Techniques: Hemming on page 22).

STEP 3

Turn the napkin over so it is wrong side up. Pin the ric rac along each edge over the sewn fold, starting a short distance from each corner and aligning it so only half of its width will show on the front to get the scalloped look. Pull the ric rac slightly to take it neatly around each corner and overlap the ends slightly. Sew the trim very close to the edge of the fabric. Press the napkin and fold to display.

lap blanket

When you are working at your desk or on the couch reading a book, having a small lap blanket that is the right size, not too big, not too small, is the perfect accompaniment to keep you warm and comfortable. And since I'm always keen to create pieces where I reuse and repurpose textiles that I find in vintage shops (or my closet), I thought, for this project, I'd try my hand at an old technique using remnants from cut up sweaters. The simple square design forms a foundation for patching a variety of knit pieces together, making a blanket that is both unique and functional.

What you need

2 or 3 wool sweaters in various colors and textures in similar weight
Grid ruler
Rotary knife
Cutting mat
Serger (overlocker)
Darning needle with a sock weight yarn in a similar color

Finished size

Approx. 30 x 40in (76 x 101.5cm)

Tips

- A medium weight of sweater will work well.
- A serger (overlocker) is only necessary to finish cut edges that won't felt – such as knits in synthetic yarn – so they don't fray or ravel, but a pure wool fabric should felt well.
- For a lap blanket roughly 30 x 40in (76 x 101.5cm) with six rows of eight squares you will need 48 pieces.

Instructions

STEP 1

Before cutting, wash all the sweaters and dry them in a tumble dryer to felt them, if possible. Using your grid ruler and rotary knife, cut your sweaters into 5 x 5in (12.5 x 12.5cm) squares.

STEP 2

Next, lay out the pieces on a table to arrange them. Try to place them in a random way but one that has a balance: spread the different varieties of knits out so that similar pieces are not all together; if there is a vertical knit pattern, every so often turn it so it's horizontal, and if there are bright colors, try to avoid them all being in one area.

STEP 3

To sew, lay two pieces together on a table, side by side. Using a darning needle threaded with sock yarn, sew the two edges together with a whip stitch (see Sewing Techniques: Whip Stitch on page 29). Be careful that your tension is not too tight or else the pieces risk becoming puckered. Make sure to tie the whip stitch at the start and end of each section. Keep adding one more square at a time until the first row is complete. Make the other rows in the same way.

STEP 4

When all rows are finished, sew each row to the next until your blanket is complete. I left the outside edge of the blanket raw, but you can work blanket stitch (see Sewing Techniques: Blanket Stitch on page 30) all around to add a finishing touch if you like.

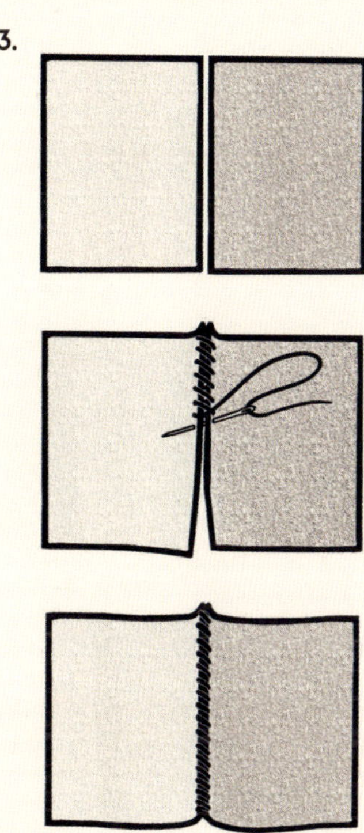

ruffled pillows

Every couch needs a pillow or two. And while I've often gravitated toward minimal gestures and natural simplicity, I have to admit that sometimes looking back to older styles, where decorative elements played a larger role, is actually a lot of fun. Ruffles are one of those elements that can add so much to your decor with whimsy and softness. This pillow design can be adapted to any shape, round or oval, and making your own is a way to play with more color and patterns, with fabric choices that are fresh and modern.

What you need

1yd (1m) of fabric
Ruler
Chalk pencil
Scissors
Serger (overlocker) (optional)
Sewing machine and thread
Zipper foot for machine if you have one
16in (40cm) zipper
Pins
Gathering foot for machine (optional)
Water-soluble marker
18 x 18in (46 x 46cm) pillow insert

Finished size

17 x 17in (43 x 43cm)

Tips

- It's best if the pillow cover is a snug fit on the pillow insert, which it will be when you have sewn the seams.

- To determine how long you need to cut the ruffle, measure the distance all around the pillow and multiply by 1.5 times. So, for a pillow with side dimensions of 18in (46cm), the ruffle fabric will be 27in (68.5cm) x 4 sides giving you a length of 108in (274cm).

- To sew through the two layers of fabric and the ruffle edge, it's advisable to use a heavier needle such as for denim.

Instructions

STEP 1

Measure and cut the pillow front to 18 x 18in (46 x 46cm), the pillow back A to 6 x 18in (15 x 46cm) and the pillow back B to 15 x 18in (38 x 46cm) – these will allow for the zipper opening.

STEP 2

If you have a serger, serge one long side on each of the zipper back pieces. If you don't have a serger, use the zigzag stitch on your machine. Place the two back pieces right sides together, with the two serged sides aligned. Sew together from each corner inwards for about 2in (5cm) or so on the serged edge only, using a ⅝in (1.5cm) seam allowance and leaving a large unsewn gap in the middle for the zipper. Press the two edges of the seam over to give the unsewn gap neat and clean folded edges.

2.

3.

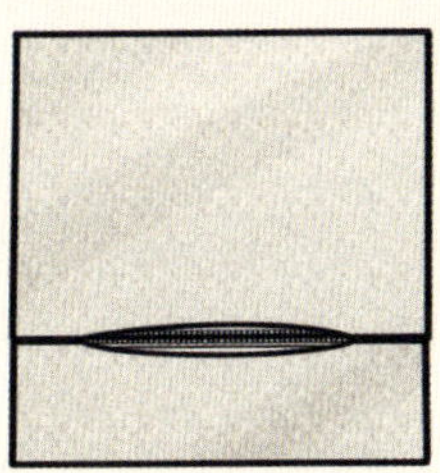

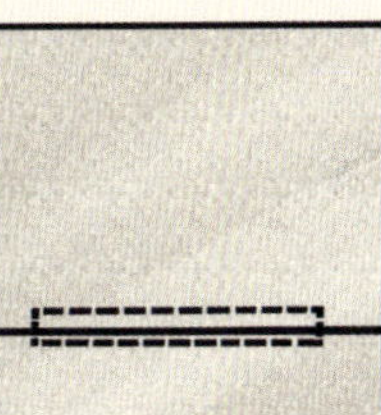

5.

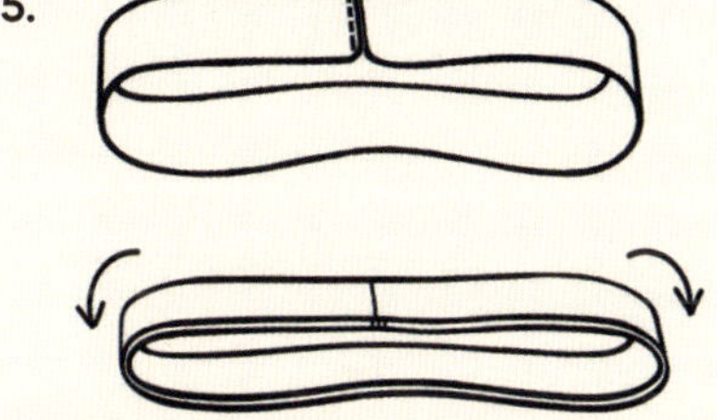

6.

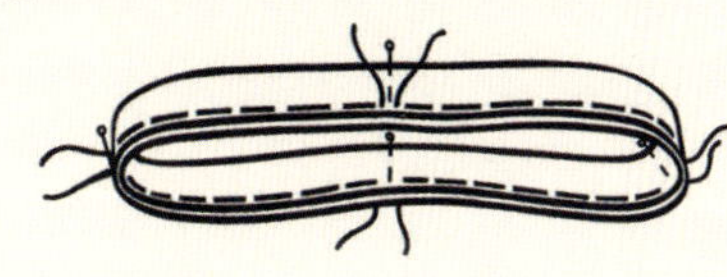

7 + 8.

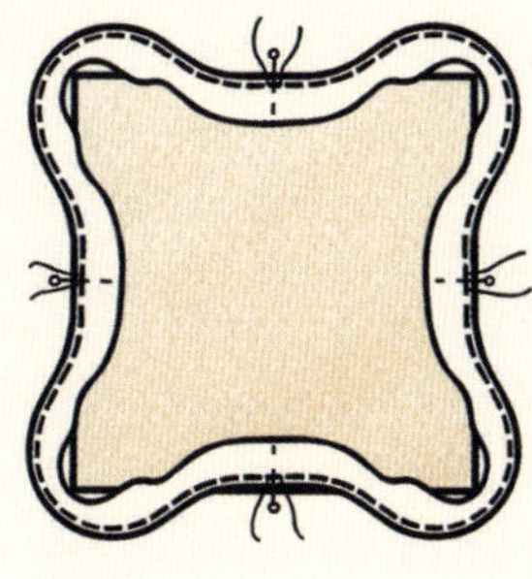

9.

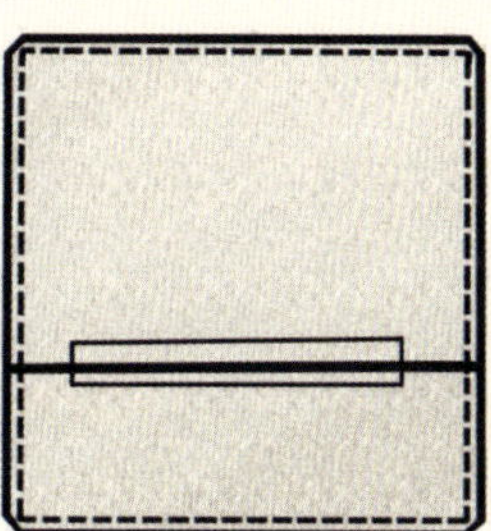

STEP 3

If you can, use a zipper foot on the machine so you can sew very close to the zipper teeth. Open out the pillow with right sides facing up and place the zipper right side up underneath the unsewn gap. Align the zipper slightly off center so the folded edge of pillow back B lies over the zipper teeth and pin in place. Working with the pillow back right side up in your machine, and with piece B at the back and piece A at the front, start by sewing the zipper across one end, then swivel to sew along the folded edge of piece A very close to the zipper teeth. Continue sewing across the opposite end and then finally along the fold of the piece B, this time sewing about ½in (1.2cm) from the zipper teeth. This will result in a flap on one side that covers the zipper from view, and you should now have a square similar in size to the front square. Set the back panel aside.

STEP 4

The ruffle strip is 5in (12.5cm) wide so that when folded and sewn you will have a ruffle that is approx. 2¼in (5.75cm) wide. Cut the fabric for the ruffle on the grain to 5 x 108in (12.5 x 274cm) – you may need to join shorter pieces of fabric to make up the length required. If so, join them right sides together with a ⅜in (1cm) seam allowance.

STEP 5

Place the two short ends of the ruffle right sides together, with edges aligned, and sew the ends together using a ⅜in (1cm) seam allowance to make the strip into a continuous loop. Then fold the fabric over lengthwise wrong sides together so that the raw edges are aligned. Press the fold and seams flat. Lastly fold the ruffle trim in half, and place a pin to mark each fold, then fold each side in half again and place two more pins to mark the additional folds. This will give four equidistant points on the entire loop.

STEP 6

If using a sewing machine, set the stitch setting for a fairly long stitch – like a basting (tacking) stitch – and sew a line of straight stitches along the raw edge of the ruffle, joining the layers together, with about a ¼in (0.6cm) seam allowance. Start each line of stitches at one of the pins and end it at the next pin, leaving lengths of thread at each point where you start and stop with no back stitching. Keep the pins in place. You will have completed a line of stitches along the entire length of the ruffle trim but in four separate sections.

STEP 7

Now, fold the pillow front in half on all four sides to find the midpoint of each side, and mark with a water-soluble marker. With the pillow front right side facing up, place the ruffle trim on top, with the raw edges aligned to the pillow front edges and the fold of the ruffle towards the inside. Secure the four pins on the ruffle trim to four midpoints of the pillow front. This will ensure that the ruffle trim is evenly distributed (the corners will extend beyond at this stage).

STEP 8

Gently, but firmly, pull one of the loose ends of thread with one hand, while ruffling the fabric along the thread with the other, to create even ruffles along one quarter of the pillow front, and making sure not to pull the thread out on either end. It may take some coaxing, but working in small sections, adjusting the folds and pinning them down as you go will help. Work from one quarter to the next until the entire trim is ruffled and fits within the raw edge of the pillow front. Sew all around, basting the ruffles down to the pillow front with a small seam allowance.

STEP 9

Place the fabric back right side down on top of the front/ruffles, with all edges aligned (the ruffles will still be facing in at this point, between the two layers). Sew along all four sides with a ⅜in (1cm) seam allowance, then serge around all four sides. Turn right sides out through the zipper, making sure to push out the corners, and insert the pillow.

coasters

There are a lot of good things about small projects. They are fast and economical because they quite often require nothing more than remnants, but mostly because they can make the most commonplace items expressive. With subtle plays of color in simple four corner patchworks, these little coasters are not only useful but are visually suggestive – like mini quilts for the table with a modern, organic touch.

What you need

4in (10cm) square of linen fabric in four colors for each coaster
Muslin (calico) backing fabric or any fabric you have on hand
6in (15cm) square of low loft batting (wadding) for each coaster
5½in (14cm) diameter paper circle template (includes ⅜in/1cm seam allowance)
Water-soluble marker
Scissors
Pins
Sewing needle and Sashiko thread

Finished size

4¾in (12cm) diameter

Tips

- Each patchwork front consists of 4 colors each cut to a 3½in (9cm) square. If you are making more than one coaster it's a good idea to do your batch cutting before you begin to sew.
- You can topstitch around the edge of each coaster with your sewing machine using an off-white thread, or hand-sew topstitching with natural Sashiko thread.

Instructions

STEP 1

Lay out your fabrics so you know where each color should go before you begin sewing. Take the first two colors and lay one on top of the other, right sides together and edge aligned, and sew a straight stitch with a ⅜in (1cm) seam allowance along one edge, back stitching at both ends. Press the seam open. Repeat with the other two colors.

Lastly, place the two sewn pairs on top of each other, right sides facing, edges and seams aligned, and sew together in the same way. Press the patchwork with an iron to flatten seams and place it aside. Repeat for all the coasters.

STEP 2

Place the paper circle template on the backing fabric, trace the circle and then cut out. With the lining right side facing down, fold it in half and then once more into quarters. Place the folded lining on top of one corner of the patchwork front, so that it lines up with the seams and center point. Holding it in place, carefully unfold flat so the lining forms a circle. This will ensure that your backing is centered on the front. Pin the lining to the patchwork front and cut around the front so that both fabric pieces are circular and aligned all around with the right sides together. Place the batting underneath this pile so that it's on the wrong side of the patchwork and pin all three layers together.

STEP 3

Sew the three layers together using a ⅜in (1cm) seam allowance leaving an unsewn gap about 2in (5cm) wide somewhere along the edge. Cut off the excess batting so the edges of all three fabrics are aligned and then cut small snips into the seam allowance around the perimeter of the sewn fabrics. Turn right sides out, making sure to push the seam out all around.

STEP 4

Thread a needle and sew the gap closed using a ladder stitch (see Sewing Techniques: Ladder Stitch on page 31). Lastly, thread a needle with Sashiko thread and sew a running stitch (see Sewing Techniques: Running Stitch on page 28) all around the coaster leaving a ⅛in (0.3cm) seam allowance along the edge. If you like, you can make the stitching more visible by increasing the seam allowance around the edge to ¼in (0.6cm).

1.

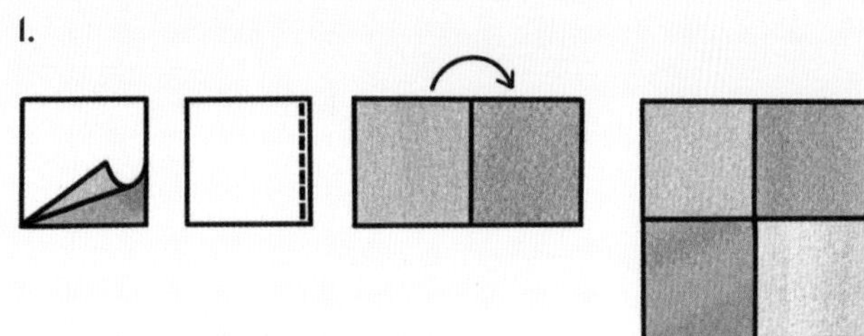

2.

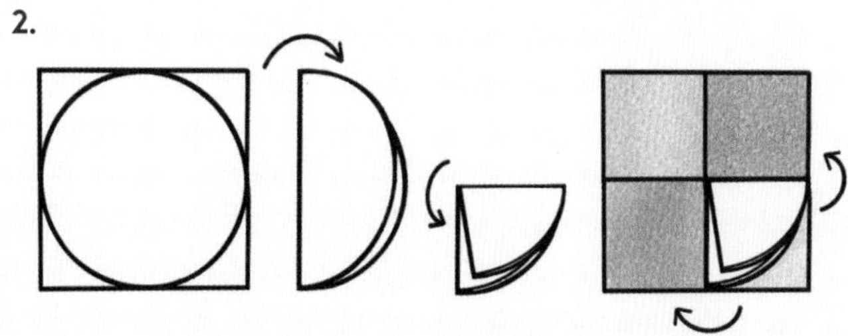

3.

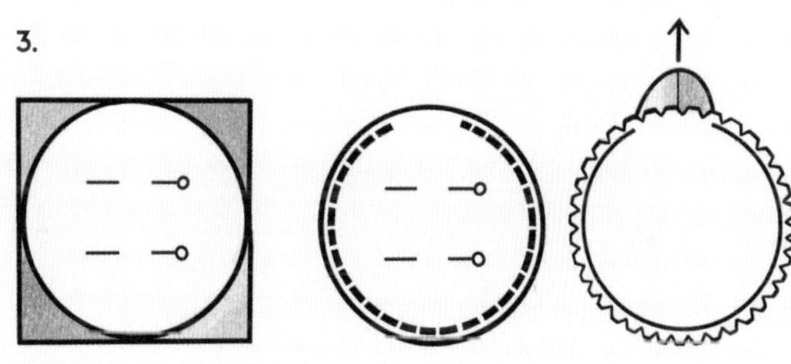

4.

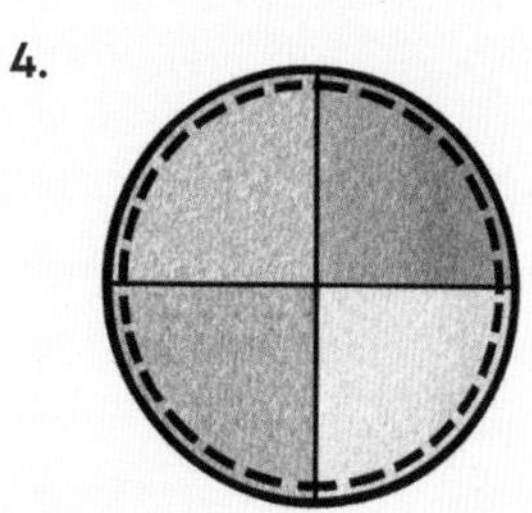

lunch bag

How can you improve the common lunch bag? A paper bag with gussets might speak of utility in its simplest form, but the great thing about making your own is that you can always add a few upgrades. This version maintains an overall simplicity but is designed with some key differences. It's made from waxed canvas, so it's reusable and easy to clean yet retains its nice sturdy shape. It has an easily folded side gusset that gives it a triangular detail and a flat bottom that allows the bag to sit upright when in use. It also has an added band at the top which forms a closure with two snaps which can be left open or rolled up, creating a small handle and making it easy to carry. Like the original, it's useful and easy to make, but this one you'll want to keep.

What you need

14 x 35in (35.5 x 89cm) of waxed canvas
3 x 18in (7.5 x 46cm) of fabric for the band
Ruler or tape measure
Sewing machine or hand sewing needle and thread
Scissors
Hera marker
Ruler
2 metal snaps (press studs) approx. ⅓in (1cm) in size

Finished size

H 14 x W 12.5 x D 5in (H 35.6 x W 31.75 x D 12.7cm)

Tips

- I used the Merchant Mills organic cotton oilskin in color Conker, 11.94oz (405gsm). This is a great weight and has a lot of structure so doesn't require a lining. Feel free to use a canvas weight fabric if you don't have waxed canvas on hand or you can use a lightweight fabric with a lining.
- As an alternative to the snaps you can also use hook-and-loop tape.

Instructions

STEP 1

Create an accordion fold at the base of the bag by first folding the fabric in half to create a line at the midpoint. Then fold one side back in the opposite direction by 2¼in (5.75cm) from the midpoint. Turn over and fold the other side over the previous two folds, 2¼in (5.75cm) from the midpoint, so that all four sides are aligned.

STEP 2

Stitch along the left and right side with a ⅜in (1cm) seam allowance, leaving the top opening unsewn.

STEP 3

Fold the edge around the top of the bag down by 1¼in (3cm) and then turn the edge under by ¼in (0.6cm). Stitch around the bag close to the folded edge so that the raw edge is inside the seam and a folded hem is made at the top that is approx. 1in (2.5cm) high. Lastly, turn the bag right sides out and push the corners out.

STEP 4

Fold the raw edge of the two short ends on the band fabric over by about ⅜in (1cm). Fold the strip in half along its entire length and then fold the raw edges on each side under by ¼in (0.6cm) so that both raw edges on the long side of the fabric are inside the fold. Sew the strip closed along all three open sides of the fabric. You don't need to sew along the top fold.

STEP 5

Place the sewn strip on one side of the bag opening so that the folded edge is aligned with the top of the bag and the two ends of the strip each protrude out from the sides by an equal distance, around 2½in (6.5cm). Use clips to hold in place.

STEP 6

Sew around the strip to the bag, close to the top and bottom edge of the strip. Make sure to also sew a vertical line of stitches along where the strip meets the side seam of the bag. Make sure to back stitch (See Sewing Techniques: Straight Stitch on page 19) at beginning and end. Once you have finished the stitching, you can add snaps onto the two ends of the strap, which will serve as the closure as well as the handle. I placed the snap holes about ½in (1.25cm) from the ends. Add the snaps according to the manufacturer's instructions, making sure that they face in opposite directions so that they meet when the bag is folded closed.

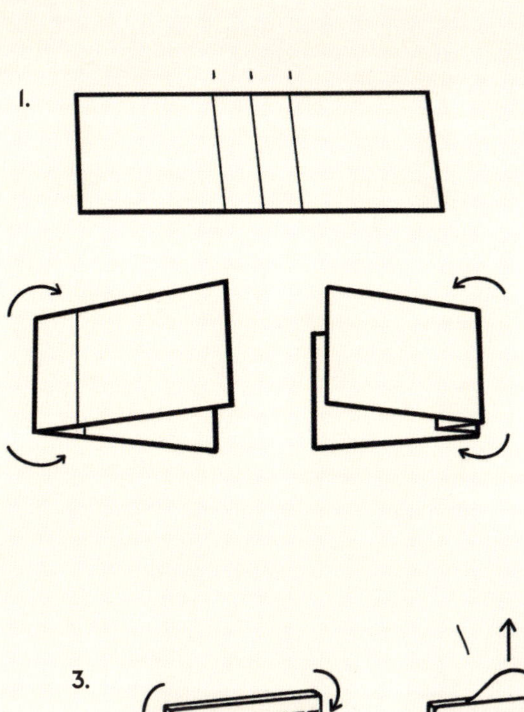
1.

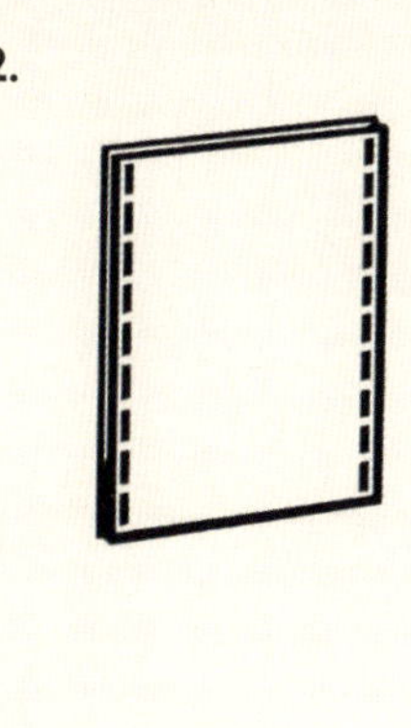
2.

3.

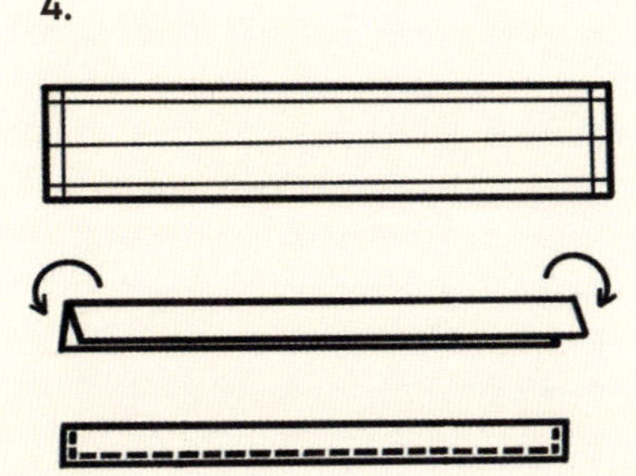
4.

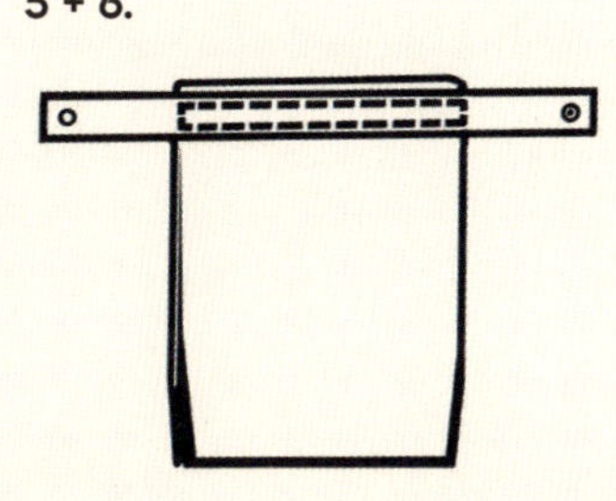
5 + 6.

utensil holder

Taking your own utensils to a picnic always makes it seem a little more special, but why not treat our daily lunch break in the same way, or even when grabbing some takeaway – or leftovers for that matter. This utensil holder is modeled on a tool holder – which makes sense since utensils are tools – and is made to be handy and portable, keeping everything you need at your fingertips. And it allows you to avoid disposable items, which is especially good when it is a daily occurrence. The holder is made of waxed canvas, which is water resistant and can be wiped over easily. It's designed with a flap to keep your utensils in place and has room for a few other things. The holder will lay flat when you are using it and easily rolls up to fit in your lunch bag or purse.

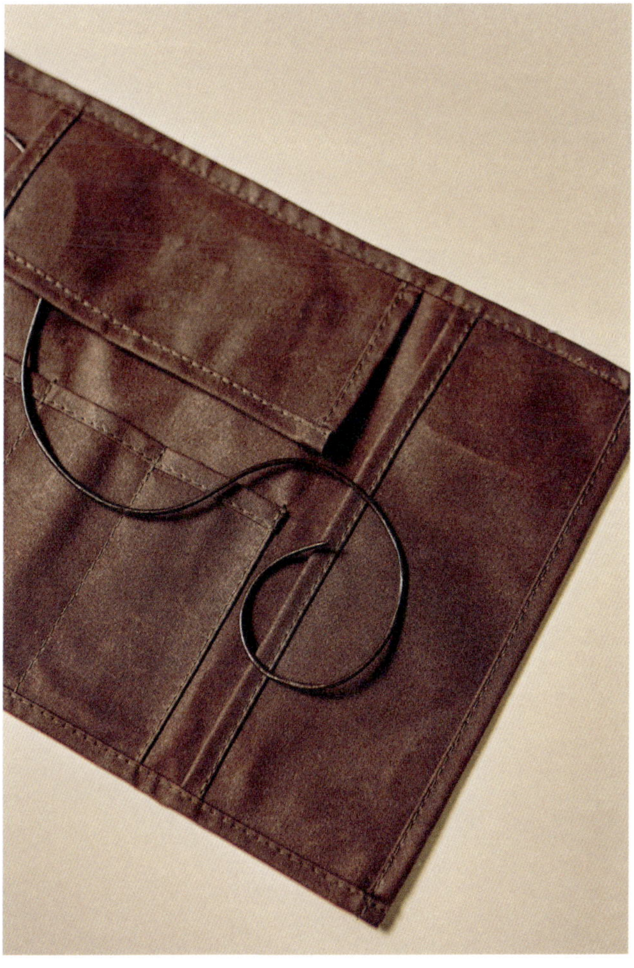

What you need

Approx. 20 x 14in (51 x 35.5cm) of cotton oilskin
Ruler
Scissors
Sewing machine and thread
Fabric clips
Hera marker
¼in (0.6cm) metal grommet with fixing kit
20in (51cm) leather cord

Finished size

8 x 11in (20 x 28cm)

Tips

- For this project I used the Merchant Mills organic cotton oilskin in color Conker, 11.94oz (405gsm). I find this to be a great weight – it's relatively thin, but with a structure that doesn't require lining.

- Don't use pins on this fabric because they will leave a permanent mark – use fabric clips instead.

Instructions

STEP 1

Cut all your fabric into four pieces as follows, which include seam allowances:

- A. Body: 9 x 12in (23 x 30cm)
- B. Napkin slot: 3½ x 8in (9 x 20cm)
- C. Utensil flap: 3½ x 7in (9 x 18cm)
- D. Utensil holder: 4½ x 6in (11.5 x 15cm)

This design is easily adaptable – you can choose to make it taller or longer, following the same construction methods.

STEP 2

Make a rolled hem on one long side of sections B and D by folding the fabric edge under by ¼in (0.6cm) and then fold one more time to make a nice, tight hem (see Sewing Techniques: Hemming on page 22). Sew along the bottom fold. Also sew a rolled hem along three sides of section C, leaving one long side unsewn.

STEP 3

Place the pieces on top of section A as shown in the diagram, making sure that you place each piece ⅝in (1.5cm) from the outside edge of A. Use fabric clips to hold the pieces in place. Fold under the two sides of section D by about ¼in (0.6cm). Place section D so that there is about ½in (1.25cm) distance between sections D and B.

STEP 4

Sew down the two sides on D close to the edge. Next measure to divide section D into three even sections, marking the lines with a Hera marker. Sew along the two marked lines, creating three even slots that will hold your utensils. Feel free to change the dimensions based on what you will be carrying. Make sure to back stitch (see Sewing Techniques: Straight Stitch on page 19) at the top of the pockets.

STEP 5

To turn under all four sides of section A, start at a corner and fold the fabric under twice ¼in (0.6cm) and then fold one more time so the raw edge is concealed, and the top edge of the hem sits on top of the other three sections. Hold in place with clips. Sew along the rolled hem all around, making sure to keep your stitch close to the folded edge.

STEP 6

Mark the center of the left side and punch a small hole about ¼in (0.6cm) from the hem. Fix a small grommet into the hole according to the manufacturer's instructions. Tie a knot at the end of the leather cord then pull the other end through the grommet. If you would rather use fabric as a tie, you can do that without using a grommet – while you are making the hem along the left side, insert the end of a fabric tie into the seam before sewing the hem.

2.

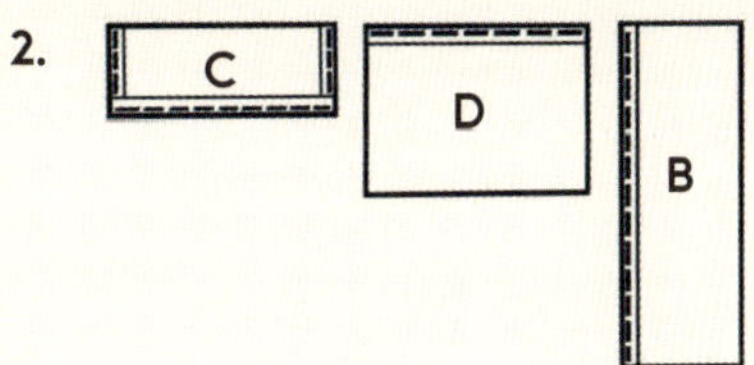

3.

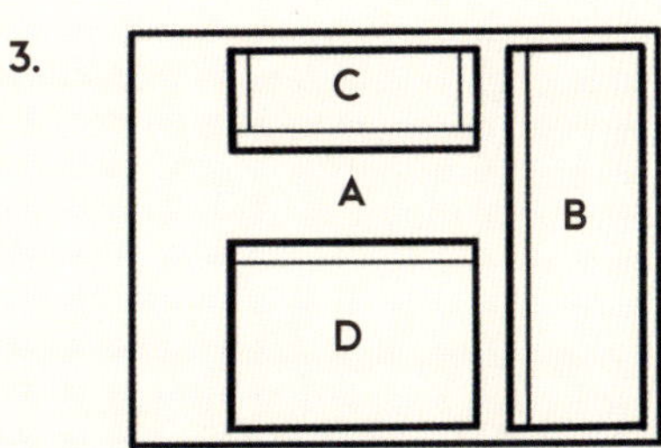

4.

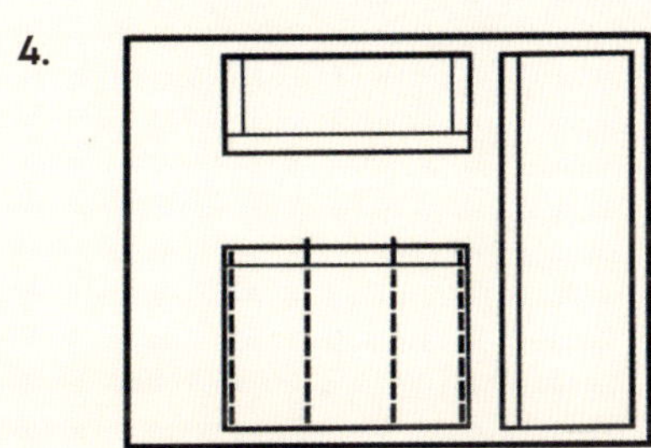

5.

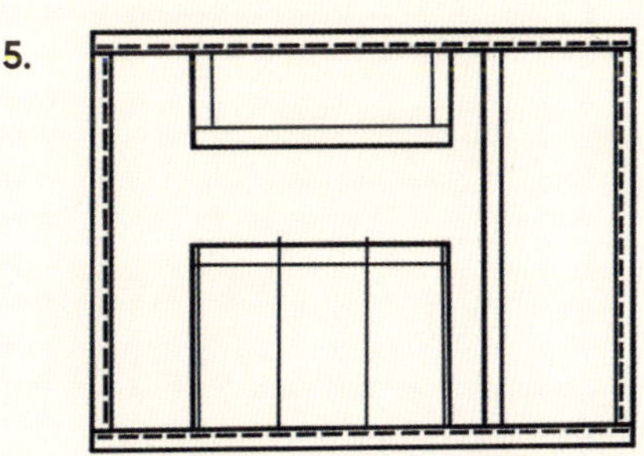

6.

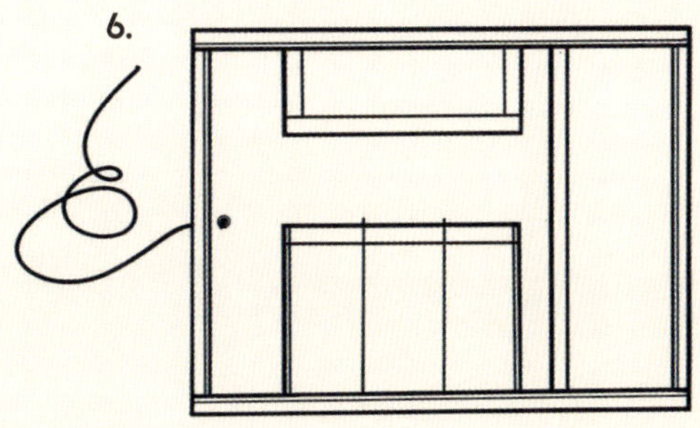

hot water bottle cover

I can't think of anything cozier than warming up with a hot water bottle – except perhaps a hot water bottle with a quilted cover. And while comfort is the focus of this project, the fabric pattern and stitching, which is reminiscent of actual quilts, makes it perfect for any decor. I used a standard 4¼ pint (2 litre) hot water bottle as a template for this removable cover, but because you will make your own template you can adjust the size for any hot water bottle you currently have.

What you need

Approx. ½yd (50cm) of printed cotton at least 36in (90cm) wide
Approx. ½yd (50cm) of muslin (calico) at least 36in (90cm) wide
Approx. 12 x 24in (30 x 61cm) of batting (wadding)
2 pieces of binding each approx. 1½ x 11in (4 x 28cm)
1 x 4in (2.5 x 10cm) of fabric for button loop
Hot water bottle
Paper for template
Pencil
Grid ruler
Scissors
Pins
Water-soluble marker
Sewing machine and thread
Serger (overlocker) (optional)
Button
Sewing needle and thread

Finished size

To fit any hot water bottle

Tips

- The fabric I used is a printed cotton/linen blend for the outside, front and back; a muslin for the lining, front and back; and a low loft cotton batting in between, front and back.

- The binding is only for straight edges so does not need to be cut on the bias. I cut mine from the printed cotton, but you could use bought bias binding.

- If you don't want to use fabric for the button loop, you can use 4in (10cm) of elastic cord or hook-and-loop tape.

- If you don't have a serger, use a zigzag stitch on your sewing machine instead.

Instructions

STEP 1

Place your hot water bottle on top of the paper and trace around it with a pencil. Expand the drawing by adding a ¾in (2cm) seam allowance all around. At the neck of the water bottle I made the seam allowance 1in (2.5cm) on either side of the spout. You may have to adjust this based on the weight of the fabric you use. Cut out the template. This will be the template for the front.

STEP 2

Place the template onto a second piece of paper and trace the top 7in (18cm), then draw a straight line across the bottom. Set aside. Finally trace the bottom 9½in (24cm), then draw a straight line across the top. These two templates are for the back – when placed on top of the front template the straight edges should overlap by at least 1in (2.5cm).

1 + 2.

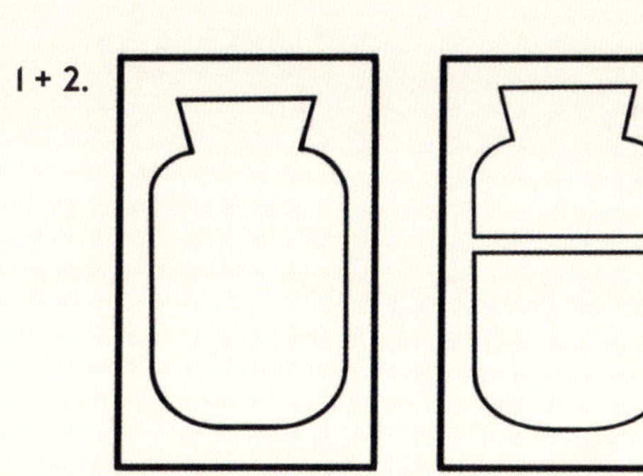

3 + 4.

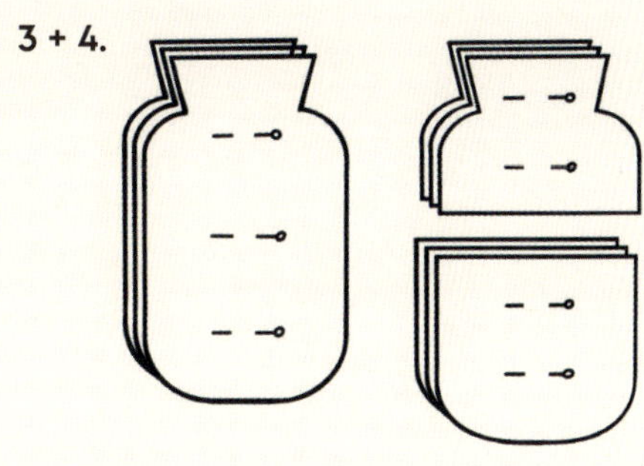

5.

7 + 8.

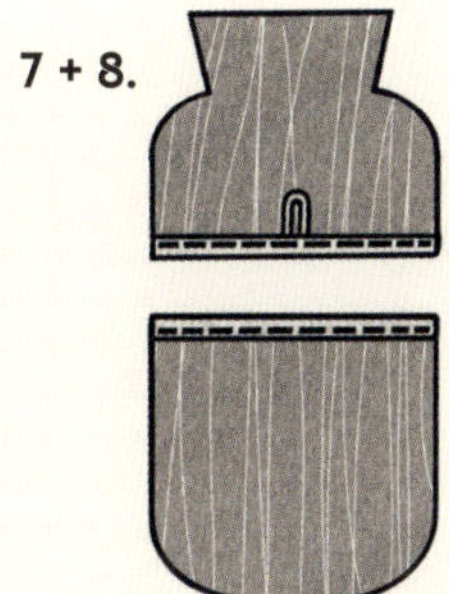

9.

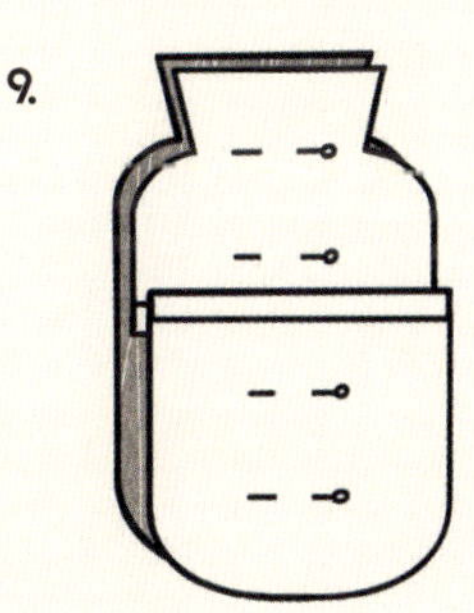

10.

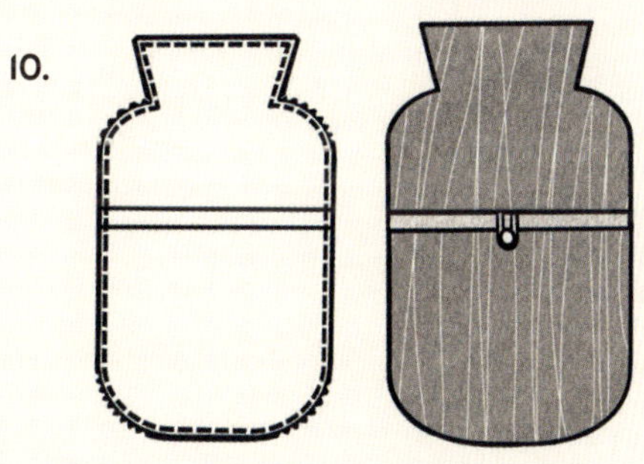

11.

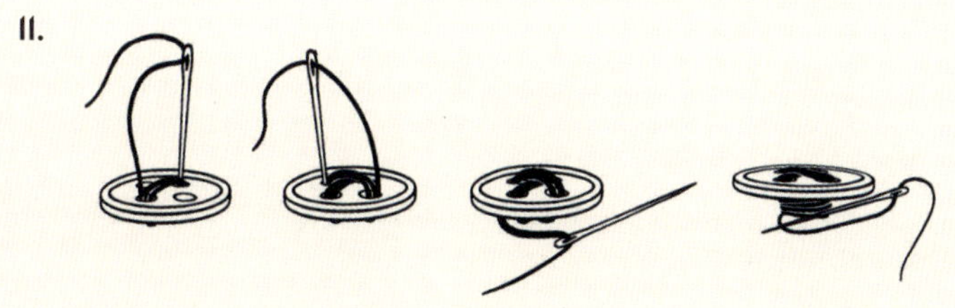

STEP 3

Cut out one piece each of the outside fabric, lining fabric and batting using the front template. Place the lining right side down, add the batting on top then the outside fabric right side up, with all edges aligned. Pin the pieces together.

STEP 4

Cut out one piece each of the outside fabric, lining fabric and batting using the top back template and the same with the bottom back template. On each set place the lining right side down, add the batting on top then the outside fabric right side up, with all edges aligned. Pin the pieces together.

STEP 5

I used a sewing machine to create quilting across the entire surface of each piece – I first drew wavy guidelines with the water-soluble marker to suggest movement, but straight lines will do as well.

STEP 6

Finish by serging each set of three layers together around the entire edge. I like to do it at this step on separate pieces because serging the three layers is doable but doing six layers of the front and back will be quite challenging.

STEP 7

Place one of the binding strips right sides together along the straight edge of the bottom back panel with edges aligned. Sew across with an allowance of ⅜in (1cm). Turn the strip right over the edge and fold under once more so that the raw edge is tucked under. Use a ladder stitch (see Sewing Techniques: Ladder Stitch on page 31) to sew the binding along the folded edge.

STEP 8

To create the button loop, fold the strip of fabric in half lengthwise and then fold in the two edges and sew along the open long edge to close it. Add the binding strip to the top back straight edge as in step 7, but before sewing the binding down on the inside fold the button loop in half and tuck the ends into the binding at the center of the edge. Sew the binding down with ladder stitch as before, catching the button loop at the same time. The button loop will be facing away from the straight edge when you finish, so fold it over and sew it to point down at the edge.

STEP 9

Place the front piece right side up on your worktable. Place the top back on top of the front with right sides together and edges aligned around the top, then place the bottom back right sides together with bottom edges aligned. At this stage the bottom back will overlap the top back. Pin in place and then sew around the perimeter using a ⅜in (1cm) seam allowance.

STEP 10

Snip across the top corners as well as at the bottom of the neck. Turn right side out through the opening in the back and push out all the corners. Now the top back will overlap the bottom back.

STEP 11

Finish by sewing a button on the back (see Sewing Techniques: Sewing a Button on page 33) just underneath the loop.

pouf

Most types of furniture have a fairly specific purpose. Not so much for poufs; they are by definition multipurpose – a seat or footrest, a stool, or even a table if you add a tray. Or just a big cushion. Which is why, perhaps, they are considered accent pieces. This one is all of the above plus one more: it's designed to be filled with anything you have on hand, such as blankets, clothing, or extra fabric. In other words it's a storage container, too. And because it's an accent piece, the fabric you choose for it can be quiet and reserved, or bright and outgoing. It's up to you.

What you need

2 pieces of fabric cut to 21in (53.5cm) diameter
2 pieces fabric for side panels cut to 15 x 33½in (38 x 85cm)
Serger (overlocker) (optional)
12in (30cm) zipper
Sewing machine and thread
Zipper foot for machine if you have one
Grid ruler
Scissors

Finished size

Approx. 20in (51cm) diameter x 14¼in (36cm) high

Tip

- The fabric I used is a medium-weight cotton/poly blend Jacquard. If you plan to use something rather lighter you might need to add an iron-on interfacing to the wrong side of each piece before sewing to help with structure and construction.

Instructions

STEP 1

Serge all the fabric edges before sewing. If you don't have a serger, use a zigzag stitch on your sewing machine.

STEP 2

Place the two side panels right sides together with edges aligned. Sew together on one short edge from both corners inwards for about 2in (5cm) or so, using a seam allowance of ⅝in (1.5cm), leaving a large unsewn gap in the middle for the zipper. Press the edges of the seam over to give the unsewn gap neat and clean edges.

STEP 3

Use a zipper foot on your machine if you have one so you can get the foot very close to the zipper teeth. Open out the sides with right sides facing up and place the zipper right side up underneath the unsewn gap (see Sewing Techniques: Sewing a Zipper on page 27). Align the zipper slightly off center so one side lies over the zipper teeth and pin in place. With the side panel right side up in your machine, start by sewing the zipper across one end, then sew along the folded edge of one side very close to the zipper teeth. Continue sewing across the opposite end and then finally along the fold of the second side, this time sewing about ½in (1.2cm) from the zipper teeth. This will result in a flap on this side that covers the zipper from view. Alternatively, you could omit the zipper but leave the opening to stuff the pouf with fabric filler at the end and sew it closed using a ladder stitch (see Sewing Techniques: Ladder Stitch on page 31).

STEP 4

Now fold the side panel so it is right sides together and the other two short edges are aligned. Sew the short sides together using a ¾in (2cm) seam allowance. Do not turn right side out yet.

STEP 5

With one of the round pieces right sides together with the side panel, pin the edges together with the round piece on top. Sew all around the perimeter using a ⅜in (1cm) seam allowance, back stitching at start and finish. Open the zip slightly. Repeat to join the other edge of the side panel to the second round piece. Clip into the seam allowances around the edge of the top and bottom to reduce bulk. Turn right sides out through the zip when completed. Stuff the pouf with anything you wish, and you can begin using it.

2.

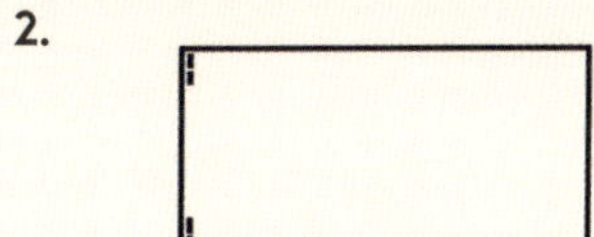

3.

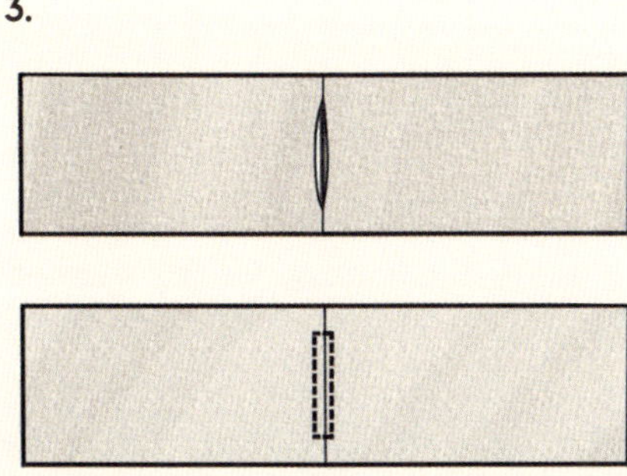

4.

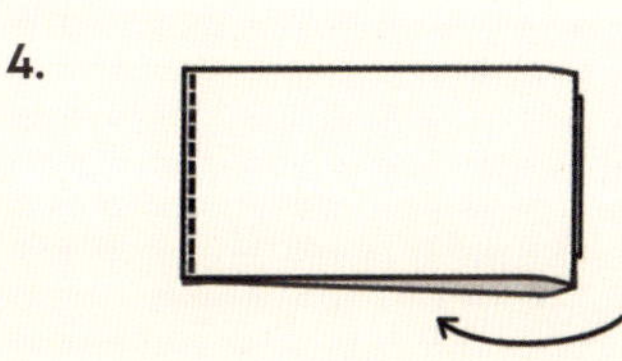

5.

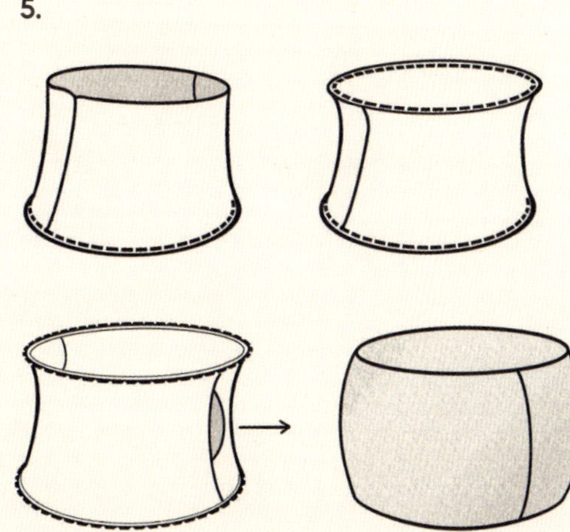

quilted oven mitt

Everyone with a kitchen needs an oven mitt, which is why they are so easy to find – but they are mostly rather generic despite an array of styles, colors, and materials. But one oven mitt you won't find in your local shop is one made by you; and making the things that you need is always gratifying. Not only is this one made with a unique patchwork and quilt stitching, but it is also something that you can customize and coordinate with your kitchen. And, of course, by using remnant fabric, it costs very little to make.

What you need

½ yd (50cm) assorted cotton fabrics
4 pieces of low-med loft cotton batting (wadding) each 10 x 14½in (25.5 x 36cm)
4 pieces of 975 insul-fleece each 10 x 14½in (25.5 x 36cm)
4 pieces of lining fabric each 10 x 14½in (25.5 x 36cm)
2 pieces of binding or bias tape, each approx. 2 x 20in (5 x 51cm)
Paper for template and pencil
Grid ruler
Scissors
Sewing machine and thread
Iron
Water-soluble marker
Pins
Off-white Sashiko thread

Finished size

7½ x 13½in (19 x 34.25cm)

Tips

- Insul-fleece is a type of batting that is used between the cotton batting and lining for heat-reflection.
- If you don't have Sashiko thread you could topstitch using your sewing machine.
- I used muslin (calico) for the lining, but feel free to use any fabric you would like.

Instructions

STEP 1

Cut the cotton fabric for the outside into 3in (7.5cm) squares – you will need at least 96 squares. Arrange the squares into four rectangles of four squares across by six squares high – you need two rectangles for each mitt.

STEP 2

Place the first two squares right sides together with edges aligned and sew along one edge with a ⅜in (1cm) seam allowance. Repeat to add the next two squares and continue until you have six rows of four squares, then sew the rows together in the same manner. Press the seams open with an iron. Repeat to make four patched panels each approx. 10 x 14½in (25.5 x 36cm).

STEP 3

To make a template for your oven mitt draw the shape around your hand, or draw around an existing oven mitt. Add a 1½in (4cm) seam allowance and cut the template out. Place it on top of the right side of one patched panel and trace around it using a water-soluble marker. Draw a second one the same way, then flip the template over to draw two more that are a mirror image to create both sides of the mitts.

STEP 4

Place each patched panel right side up on top of a piece of batting and pin together. Using your grid ruler, draw a line down and across in the middle of the fabric pieces, then repeat to draw a grid of lines.

STEP 5

With Sashiko thread and a needle, stitch along the drawn lines using a running stitch (see Sewing Techniques: Running Stitch on page 28). This will keep the layers together as well as provide padding. Make sure to stop stitching when you reach the edge of the template outline and finish by tying a knot underneath. When all the stitching is finished, trim all the layers to the outline of the mitt template. Repeat for the remaining panels.

STEP 6

Place the panels right sides together to make a pair of mitts, then sew around using a ⅜in (1cm) seam allowance but leaving the bottom edge unsewn. Snip into the seam allowance along the curves and in the space between the thumb and fingers area. Turn the mitt right side out. Spritz with a little water so that the water-soluble lines will disappear.

STEP 7

Use the oven mitt template to cut out four pieces of lining fabric, again flipping the template if there is a right and wrong side to get two opposite pairs. Place a piece of insul-fleece on the wrong side of each lining fabric piece and pin in place. Place a pair of linings on top of each other right sides together and sew all around the edge using a ⅜in (1cm) seam allowance, but leaving the bottom edge unsewn. Snip into curves and the space between the thumb and fingers as before.

STEP 8

Slide a lining inside each mitt. Sew the outer and inner layers together all around the unsewn edge of the bottom of the mitt, very close to the edge, then trim any extra fabric to around 1⁄16in (0.15cm) from the seam.

STEP 9

Align one edge of the binding right sides together along the bottom of an oven mitt and pin. Fold the beginning end over on top, then sew the binding to the oven mitt all around with a ½in (1.25cm) seam allowance, overlapping the final end as you stop (see Sewing Techniques: Binding an Edge Method One on page 23). Fold the binding over the bottom edge to the inside, then fold one more time to turn the raw edge of the trim underneath. Sew down with a ladder stitch (see Sewing Techniques: Ladder Stitch on page 31). Repeat for the other mitt.

2.

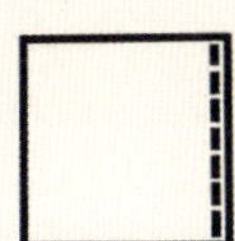

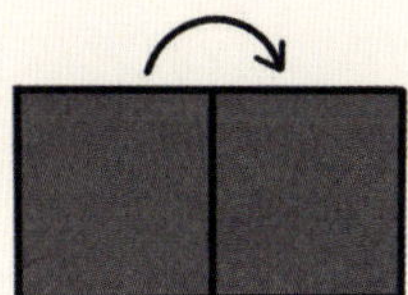

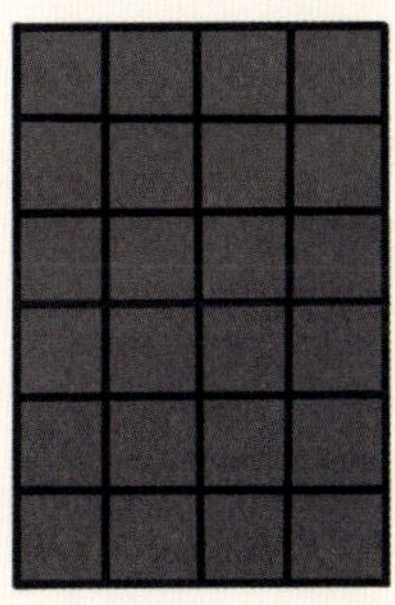

4.

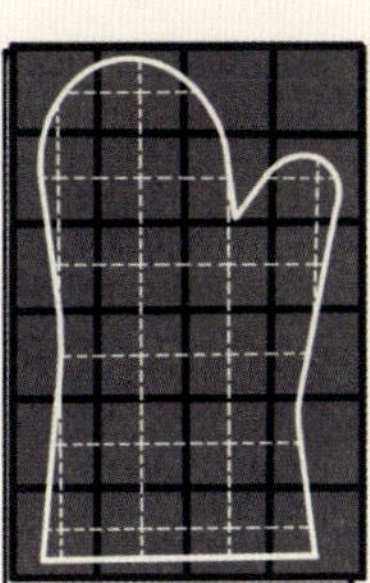

5.

6.

8.

9.

woven trivet

Having lots of trivets available for any table setting is important, especially fabric ones that are so versatile – you can leave them on the table, stack them up, or store them in a drawer without the fuss of solid trivets. This is a simple project and another way to use up small bits of fabric that you have left over. I like the way printed fabrics, when cut up and woven, have a nice balance between image and pattern. Try it with various patterns and colors to create a set of different trivets.

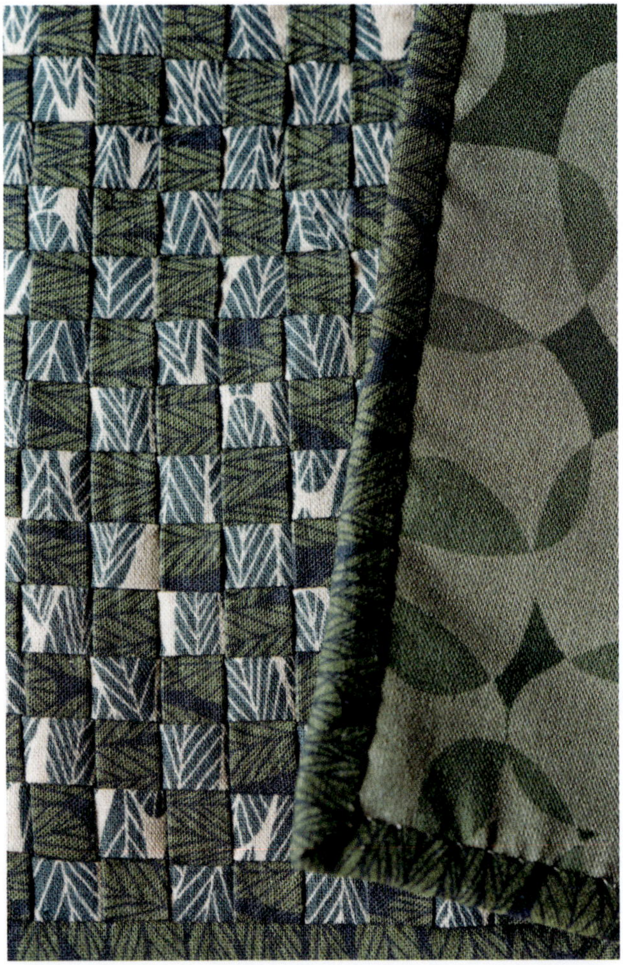

What you need

18 strips of fabric, each 2 x 14in (5 x 35.5cm) for color 1
18 strips of fabric, each 2 x 14in (5 x 35.5cm) for color 2
14 x 14in (35.5 x 35.5cm) of foam core
1 x 44in (2.5 x 112cm) of binding fabric
10½ x 10½in (26.75 x 26.75) of backing fabric
10½ x 10½in (26.75 x 26.75) of low loft batting (wadding)
Bias tape maker that makes ½in (1.25cm) on single fold (optional)
Iron
Pins
Scissors
Masking tape

Finished size

10 x 10in (25.5 x 25.5cm)

Tips

- I used a medium weight cotton/linen blend with a similar print in two different colors for the front strips and bias, and a plain cotton for the back.
- Don't cut the fabric strips for the woven section on the bias, because you don't want them to stretch. But if you have a bias tape maker, and iron as you fold, this will speed up the process.

Instructions

STEP 1

Fold the edges of each fabric strip to the middle with wrong sides together. Press the folds in place. If you have a bias tape maker it will fold the fabric strip as you pull it through, so you just need to press the folds.

STEP 2

Take the strips of color 1 and line them up right next to each other on your sewing machine table, with one end aligned and with the right side facing up and the folded side facing down. One by one, sew across the end of each strip in order, joining them together ⅛in (0.3cm) from the edge, making sure to back stitch (see Sewing Techniques: Straight Stitch on page 19) at the beginning and the end. You now have all the color 1 strips sewn together along just one ends.

STEP 3

Place the sewn strips onto the foam core, with the sewn line at the top and the strips hanging vertically, and place pins into the foam core at an angle along the top and at left and right corners to hold it in place. These strips will be the warp.

STEP 4

Begin weaving the strips together. First, fold back every other strip of color 1 on the foam core. Then lay one strip of color 2 horizontally on top, with right side facing up and tight against the top. Let the strip extend beyond on both sides and hold it in place with a pin on both ends. These horizontal strips will be the weft.

STEP 5

Bring down all the strips of the warp, color 1, that you had folded back, and lay them on top of the horizontal strip of color 2. Make sure all the strips are snugly in place and that there are no gaps in between.

STEP 6

Repeat steps 4 and 5, alternating the strips of the warp that are folded up with each horizontal weft strip you place down, so that all strips are woven, under and over, and you have a complete square with an even number of warp and weft strips.

STEP 7

Once the weaving is complete, place masking tape on top of the weaving along the three unsewn edges to stabilize them. Take the pins out and remove the weaving from the foam core. Sew along the remaining three unsewn sides along the edge of the last strip. Trim off any of the strips that extend beyond, being mindful not to cut the lines of stitches.

STEP 8

Place the lining right side down. Place the batting on top then the woven panel right side up. Pin all three layers in place and trim any batting and lining so that all three edges are aligned. Place the binding strip right sides together on top of the weave and sew around the perimeter using a ⅜in (1cm) seam allowance, making mitered corners (see Sewing Techniques: Binding All Around with Mitered Corner on page 25). Fold the binding over to the wrong side, then fold over again making sure the raw edge is inside the fold and the corners on the back are mitered as well. Pin in place and then use a ladder stitch (see Sewing Techniques: Ladder Stitch on page 31) to sew down the edge.

1.

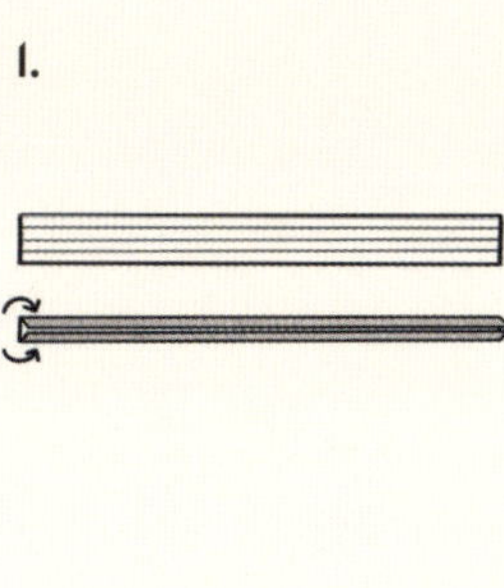

2.

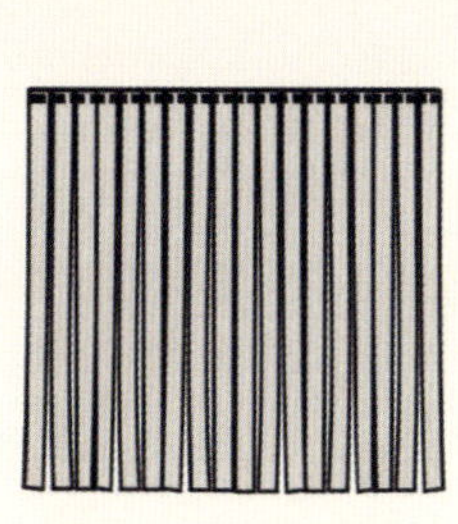

3.

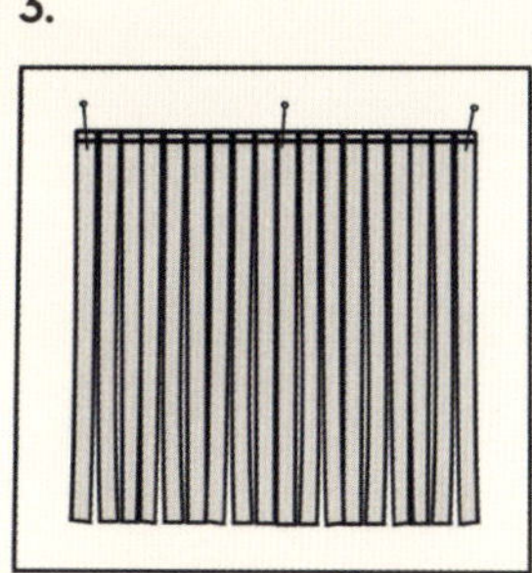

4.

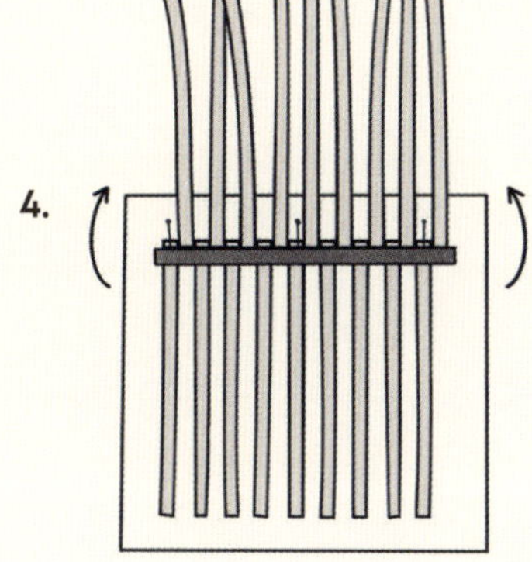

5.

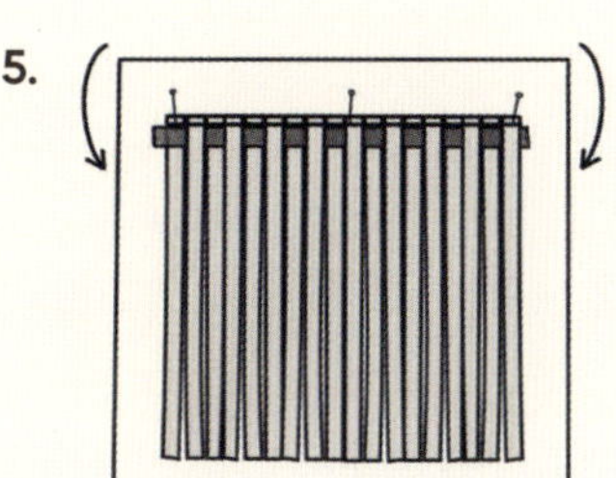

6.

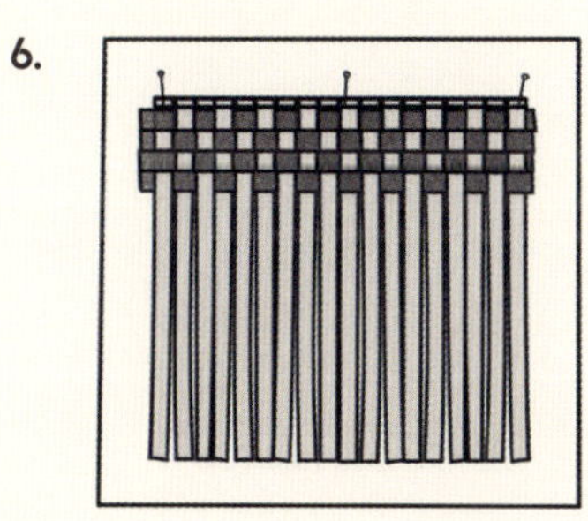

7.

8.

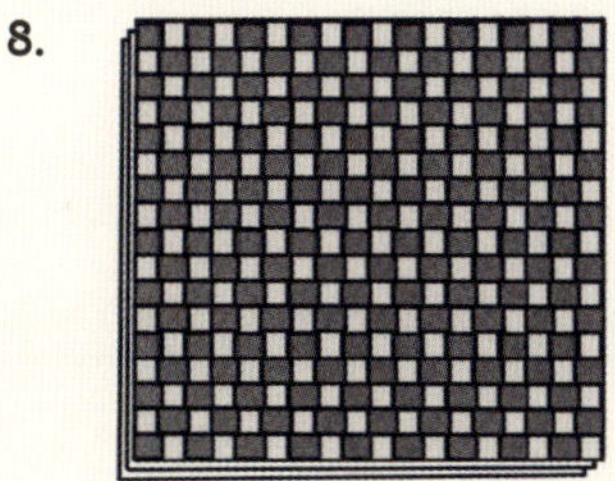

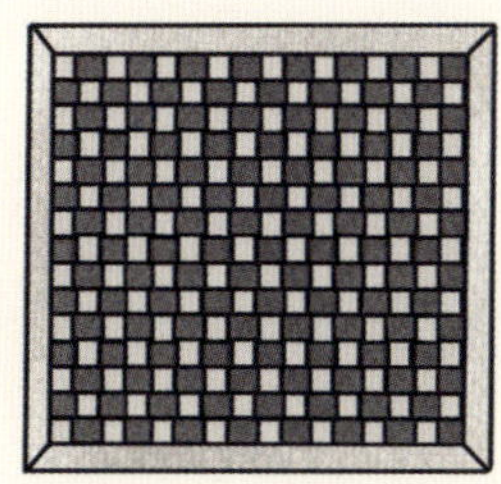

cook´s apron

Some aprons are made with large pieces of fabric, but for this one I wanted to use smaller leftover pieces that I already had. For this design there is a longer centerpiece panel with smaller ones on either side and with pockets that are integrated with the seam. The pieces that I used have a consistent pattern, but you could easily take advantage of center panel and wings of this design to play with multiple prints or colors. The apron can also be easily adapted for your body type.

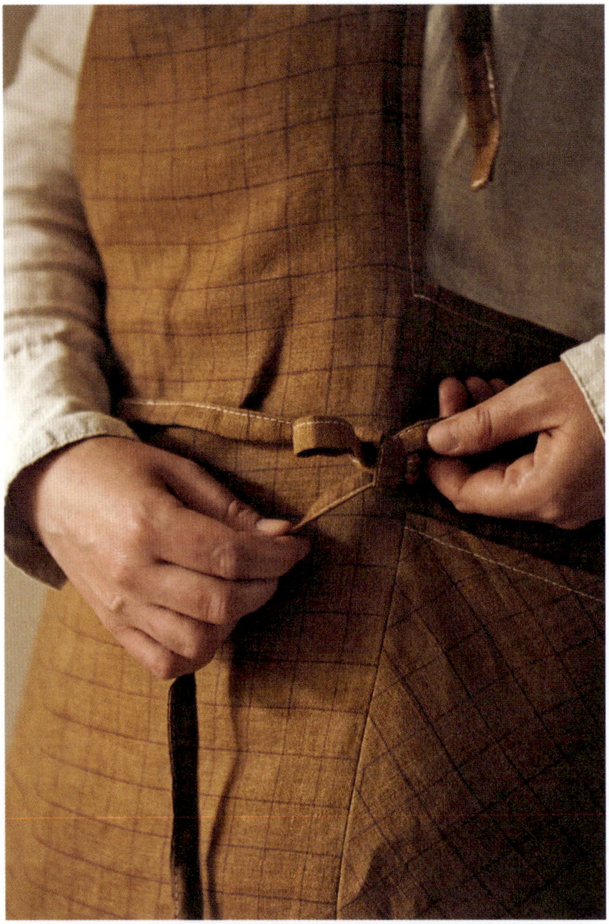

What you need

Approx. 2¼yd (2m) of linen at least 36in (90cm) wide
Tape measure
Grid ruler
Water-soluble marker
Scissors
Serger (overlocker) (optional)
Sewing machine and thread

Finished size

Body approx. 46in (117cm) wide x 33in (84cm) high not including straps

Tips

- I used a medium weight linen fabric for all pieces.
- Since there are multiple panels that are identical to each other, R or L will be added to their reference letter in step 2 to indicate which side of the apron (right or left) you are working on, if looking at the apron from the front.
- The pockets can be cut on the bias, to add some extra detail to the design.
- The design can be easily modified to be made longer or wider; just modify the dimensions according to your needs.

Instructions

STEP 1

Start by cutting all your pieces to the dimensions provided.

- Center panel A, 13 x 34in (33 x 86.5cm)
- 2 side panels BL+BR, each 18 x 24in (46 x 61cm)
- 2 pockets CL+CR, each 10 x 12in (25.5 x 30cm)
- 2 waist ties, each 2 x 38in (5 x 96.5cm)
- 2 neck ties, each 30in (5 x 76cm)
- 2 neck tie loops, each 4in (5 x 10cm)

STEP 2

Serge on the two long sides of panel A. If you don't have a serger, use a zigzag stitch on your sewing machine instead. For panels B, serge BL on the long right side, and serge BR on the long left side. For the pockets C, serge CL on the short right side, and serge CR on the short left side.

STEP 3

On each pocket create a ⅝in (1.5cm) hem on the top long edge by folding it over twice, pressing flat with an iron, and sewing along the edge (see Sewing Techniques: Hemming on page 22). Fold the remaining two raw edges of both pockets over by ¼in (0.6cm) once, and press flat but do not fold the serged edge.

STEP 4

On pieces D, E, and F fold the raw edges under to the wrong side along their entire length, and then fold one more time so that the raw edges are hidden within the fold. For D and E make sure that one of the short ends is folded in so that there are no raw edges visible. Press with an iron and sew along the edges of the folded seam on all the pieces.

STEP 5

Place CR right side up on top of BR right side facing up and with serged sides aligned. Measure the pocket placement so that it's 5in (12.5cm) from the top of BR. Pin the pocket in place and sew around it, close to the edge, leaving the top with sewn hem unsewn. Then sew a double line on the bottom and one side edge only by lining up the sewing foot to the previous sewn line, leaving only a single line along the serged side. Repeat this on the other side with BL and CL.

STEP 6

Sew the two side panels B on either side of the center panel A. Start by placing BR right sides together on top of panel A, with the sides that are serged aligned on the right side of panel A, and flush at the bottom (this will result in a bib at the top of A). Sew along the serged edges with a ⅜in (1cm) seam allowance. Leave about ¾in (2cm) unsewn at the top of this seam so that you can roll under the hem. Repeat to sew BL onto the left side of center panel A.

STEP 7

Turn the apron over to the wrong side and create a rolled hem along the tops of both panels B. Starting on one side, fold over the top edge to the wrong side twice, tucking the raw edge into the fold, and pinning in place. Repeat on the other side. To sew, start in the corner where panels A and B meet, and sew the hem closed along the top right to the outside corner. At the corner place one of the side ties D, with stitches facing down, on top of and aligned with the hem just sewn, with the raw end pointing outwards, about ¼in (0.6cm) from the side edge of panel B.

STEP 8

Now create a hem along the sides of panel B by folding over the edge twice, tucking the raw edge and the raw end of the side tie D into the hem at the corner. Pin in place and then sew the hem from the top corner down the entire side. To finish the side, return to the corner with the side tie and fold it out over the side hem, then sew in place along the edge of the hem. Repeat steps 7 and 8 for the other side of the apron.

STEP 9

Along the side of panel A fold under the serged edge only once by ⅜in (1cm) and, starting at the top, sew down the edge with a ¼in (0.6cm) seam allowance. When you get to the corner where panel A and B meet, continue sewing any unsewn sections, and turn at the corner to meet the stitching along the top of panel B. Repeat on the other side of panel A.

STEP 10

At the top of A fold the raw edge over to the wrong side twice to make a ¼in (0.6cm) hem. Place neck tie E, with stitches facing down, on top of the hem on the side of panel A, and tuck the short raw end into the folded hem right at the corner. Sew across the top till you get to the other corner where you will fold neck tie loop F in half, tuck the raw edge into the fold of the hem and then sew to the corner. Lastly, fold E and F up and out and sew in place along the edge of the hem.

STEP 11

Finish by creating a hem along the entire bottom of panel A and both panels B by folding the edge up twice and sewing it down with a ⅜in (1cm) seam allowance.

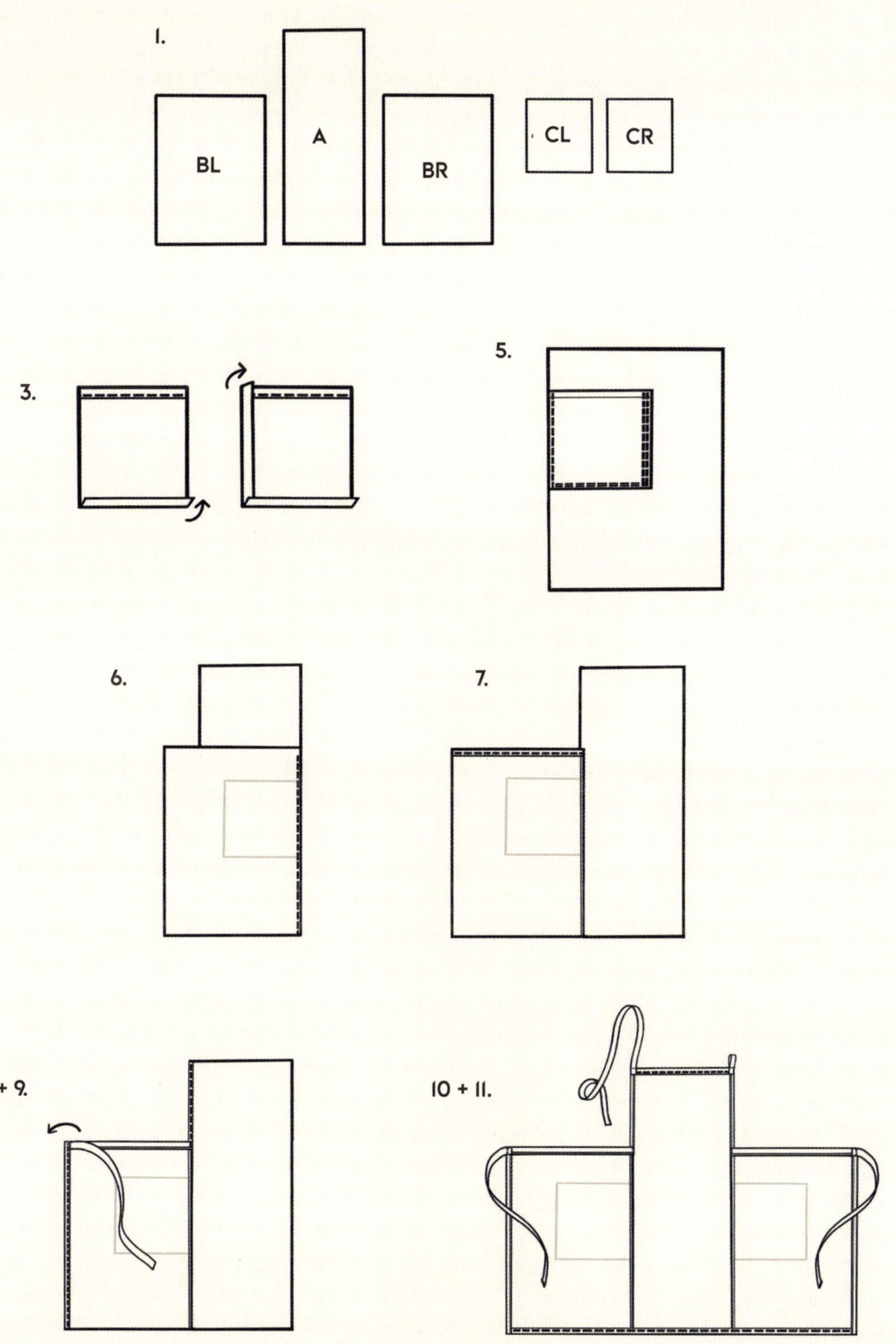
1.
BL
A
BR
CL
CR
3.
5.
6.
7.
8 + 9.
10 + 11.

waist apron

This design is an alternative to the large apron. It's great for when you are in the kitchen but also has large pockets that are good for when doing chores either in the house or in the garden. The body of the apron is made from one piece of fabric, which when folded creates the two pockets, so this project is really quick and simple to make.

What you need

Approx. 1¼yd (1.2m) of linen at least 36in (90cm) wide
Tape measure
Grid ruler
Scissors
4 x 7in (10 x 18cm) piece of cardstock
Water-soluble marker
Serger (overlocker) (optional)
Sewing machine and thread

Finished size

24 x 15in (67 x 38cm) – total strap length 88in (223.5cm)

Tip

- To avoid wasting fabric you may need to cut the waist strap in two pieces and join them to get the full length.

Instructions

STEP 1

Cut your fabric pieces to size:

- Apron body, 24 x 26in (61 x 66cm) width x height
- Waist strap 5 x 88in (5 x 223.5cm) or adjust length to fit your body
- 2 pocket bindings, each 1½ x 11in (4 x 28cm) cut on the bias
- 2 apron side bindings, each 1½ x 16in (4 x 40.5cm) cut on straight grain

STEP 2

Lay the main body of the apron on a flat work surface with the shorter width at the top. Draw a curve on the cardstock to create a template for the pocket opening. Cut along your drawn line and then place the shape onto one of the upper corners of the apron and trace the outline onto the fabric with a water-soluble marker. Turn the template over and repeat on the other upper corner. Cut the corners off along the drawn line.

STEP 3

Place the pocket edge binding right sides together on top of the apron body aligned along the curved edge and pin in place (it's fine if the binding extends beyond the apron). Sew along the binding using a ¼in (0.6cm) seam allowance. Wrap the binding over the edge to the wrong side and fold again to hide the raw edge in the fold. To secure the binding you can either sew it along the folded edge with a sewing machine or you can sew it by hand using a ladder stitch (see Sewing Techniques: Ladder Stitch on page 31). I prefer to do it by hand because I have more control smoothing the curve as I sew. Repeat these steps for the second pocket on the other side.

STEP 4

Fold the apron in half horizontally with the right sides facing out, so that the top and bottom edges are aligned along the top. Fold the apron side binding over to the wrong side at one end by about ½in (1.25cm). Place the binding right sides together on the apron, with the folded end aligned with the bottom edge, and the raw edges aligned along the side of the apron. Sew the binding down with a ⅜in (1cm) seam allowance. Then fold it over to the other side and fold one more time to hide the raw edge in the fold. Pin in place and then sew along the fold by hand with a ladder stitch or by machine.

STEP 5

Fold the waist strap in half and mark the midpoint (this might be where you joined two pieces to make up the length). Repeat with the body of the apron to find its midpoint and mark this on the top edge. Place the waist strap right sides together on top of the front of the apron, with the midpoints matching. Pin in place and then sew across the width of the apron using a ⅜in (1cm) seam allowance. Press flat with an iron, continuing the fold of the seam along both ends of the strap.

STEP 6

Fold the apron waist strap so that it's facing up and press flat with an iron. Fold the entire long unsewn edge of the waist strap by ¼in (0.6cm) to the wrong side and press in place. Then fold it in half so that the fold along the unsewn edge aligns with the sewn edge on the front. Fold the two ends in by about ½in (1.25cm), press flat with an iron, and pin in place.

STEP 7

To finish, sew along the fold from one end of the waist strap to the other to close the bottom. You can either topstitch with the sewing machine along the entire perimeter of the strap, including across the body, or sew the closure by hand using a ladder stitch along the straps, and along the back of the apron if you prefer the stitches not be visible.

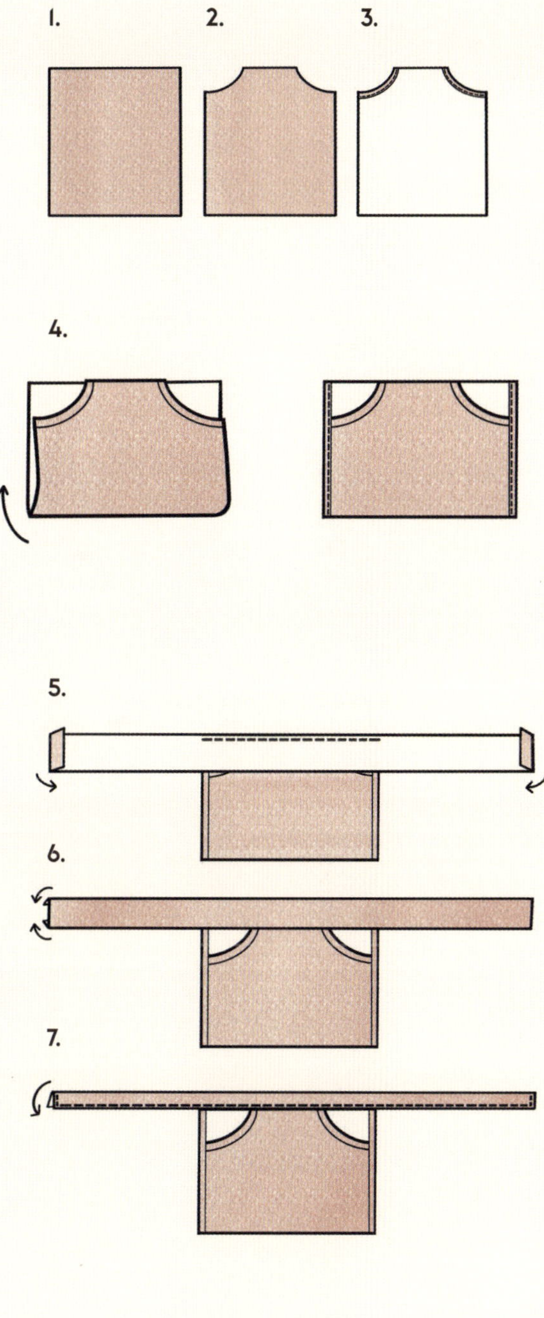

wall pocket storage

In any creative space it's easy to misplace things, which is why it's common to find tools organized on workshop walls where they are visible and easy to grab – but this is not so common in other rooms in the house. I find it particularly useful in my studio to keep some supplies and tools on hand for quick and easy access without having to search through cupboards and drawers. This wall pocket organizer can work well in any room in your home and can easily be modified to accommodate your needs by making it smaller or larger or adding more sewn lines to create more sections in the pockets. It's made of canvas for its durability and minimalist neutral tones, which won't add visual clutter in my space, but can be made from any fabric you have on hand – just add some interfacing if you're using a thinner cotton or linen. You can use nails, tacks, or hooks to hang your organizer on a wall or on the back of a door.

What you need

Approx. 2½yd (2.3m) of 8oz (227g) canvas fabric
Grid ruler
Scissors
Sewing machine and thread
Iron
Water-soluble marker
Pins

Finished size

20¼ x 34¾in (51.5 x 88cm)

Tip

- The hanging loop strip will be cut into three even lengths, or as an option you can insert grommets instead.

Instructions

STEP 1

Cut your fabric pieces to size as follows:

- A. Top pockets 21 x 6in (53.5 x 15cm)
- B. Middle pockets 21 x 8in (53.5 x 20cm)
- C. Bottom pockets 25½ x 10in (65 x 25.5cm)
- D. Tool holder 24 x 4in (61 x 10cm)
- 2 wall pocket body, each 21 x 35½in (53.5 x 90cm)
- Hanging loops, 2 x 12in (5 x 30cm)

STEP 2

For pockets A, B, and C, create a rolled hem of about ¼in (0.6cm) on one long side of each piece by folding over twice. The sides showing the hem will be the right sides, with the hem at the top. Fold tool holder D in half along the entire length and then fold the two raw edges under to the inside by ¼in (0.6cm) each. Press flat and sew closed along both folded edges – you will now have a strip that is 1¾in (4.5cm) wide. Fold loops F in half along the entire length and then fold the two raw edges under to the inside, press flat, and sew the strip closed along the folded edge. Cut F into three evenly-sized pieces.

STEP 3

Lay one panel of body E flat, right side facing up. Measure and mark the midway point along the shorter bottom edge and do the same on the bottom edge of bottom pocket C. Place C on top of E, right side facing up, aligned along the bottom edge, with both midway marks aligned. Pin in place and then stitch a vertical line at the midway point to join C to E, back stitching at the top for reinforcement. Along the bottom edge on one side of the midpoint fold C to make a gusset starting 1in (2.5cm) from the center stitches, going back to the midpoint, and then folding away again. Baste (tack) the gusset corner down with a few stitches along the bottom edge. Repeat this gusset fold on the other side of the midpoint. Flatten the pockets along the bottom edge and place a few stitches along the left and right edge to hold the pocket in place.

STEP 4

Measure a point 3½in (9cm) above bottom pocket C and mark along the left and right edges of E. At one of these side marks place the bottom edge of tool holder D, with one end aligned to the outside edge of E. Pin in place along the outside edge. Now, moving inward along D, measure about 2in (5cm) and sew a vertical line to hold the strap down. Moving inward again, this area will consist of loops large enough to hold your tools. Divide it as you wish (place an actual tool down to test how big a loop you will need), and sew vertical stitches with 1in (2.5cm) gaps between loops, finishing on the other end with a similar space of about 2in (5cm). Make sure to use the marks you made to keep the strip level. Snip off any extra fabric you didn't need.

STEP 5

Fold a ¼in (0.6cm) single fold hem to the wrong side of pocket B along the long unsewn side and iron flat. Place B on top of body E, aligned to the edge on one side and 3in (7.5cm) above the tool strip below. Pin in place and sew the hem down along the bottom edge. When done, sew a secondary stitch line by placing the edge of the sewing foot along the previous sewn line. Trim any extra fabric that extends beyond E on the other end. Divide the pocket into three equal sections and sew vertical stitches at each point, making sure to back stitch (see Sewing Techniques: Straight Stitch on page 19) at the top to secure the pocket. Leave the two outside edges unsewn.

STEP 6

Repeat step 5 with pocket A, 2in (5cm) above the top edge of pocket B, but divide this pocket into four even sections.

STEP 7

Join the two ends of each hanging loop F to form a loop and sew close to the edge to keep the shape together. Place the loops at the top of panel E making sure that they are facing down and the raw edge is along the top edge. Place one in the center and the other two ½in (1.25cm) from the right and left sides. Baste them in place with a few stitches close to the edge.

STEP 8

Place the second panel E right sides facing on top of the first and pin the two pieces together with all edges aligned. Starting at the bottom, and leaving a gap of 3in (7.5cm) so you can turn the project right sides out, sew around the perimeter with a ⅜in (1cm) seam allowance. Trim across the corners and turn the piece right side out, then press flat. Topstitch right along the edge of the piece all around – this will also close the unsewn opening on the bottom. As a final step, sew a secondary stitch line by placing the foot on the edge of the first, giving you a double stitched edge.

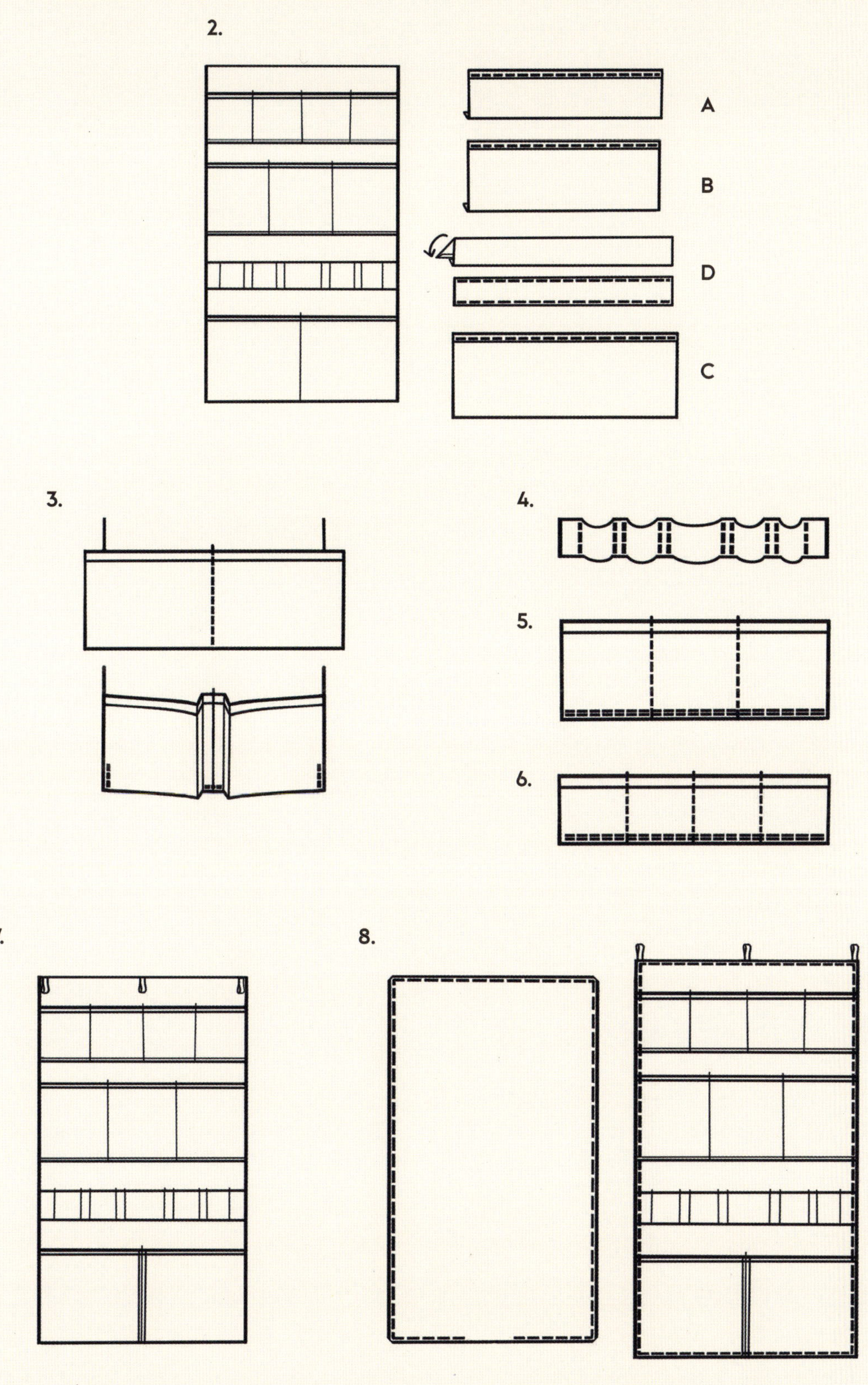
2.
A
B
D
C
3.
4.
5.
6.
7.
8.

hanging laundry bag

This hanging bag is a casual way to collect laundry without the need of a hamper taking up floor space, so it's perfect for either your bedroom, kitchen, or bathroom. The design helps to organize your home by using otherwise wasted space on a wall or behind a door. And because of that, you can use any fabric that you have on hand, or even repurposed sheets.

What you need

24 x 56in (61 x 142cm) of fabric for the body of the bag
11 x 19in (28 x 48cm) of backing fabric
Approx. 6 x 13in (15 x 33cm) of interfacing
Paper for template, large enough to cut a hole 6 x 13in (15 x 33cm)
Grid ruler
Tape measure
Scissors
Serger (overlocker) (optional)
Pins
Sewing machine and thread

Finished size

24 x 28in (61 x 71cm)

Tip

▸ Use a medium- to heavy-weight cotton or linen fabric for all parts of this project. The height of 56in (142cm) was the length of the fabric bolt, which when folded gives a finished size of 24 x 28in (61 x 71cm), with a fold at the bottom. If you don't have a large enough piece of fabric you can join two pieces of 24 x 28in (61 x 71cm) with a seam at the bottom.

Instructions

STEP 1

Serge the backing fabric around all four sides. On the template paper draw an oval approx. 6 x 13in (15 x 33cm) with round corners. Fold it in half to ensure that it is symmetrical, then cut the shape out. Place the template, centered, on the backing fabric, trace the template and then cut out an opening. Put the remnant from the cutting of this opening aside to make the two hanging loops.

STEP 2

Place the same template on top of the right side of the main piece, centered and about 4in (10cm) from the top short side. Trace the shape of the hole and cut it out (through one layer only). Put the fabric from the cutout aside.

STEP 3

Place the backing fabric right sides together on top of the main piece with the two hole cutouts aligned. Pin in place. Sew the two pieces together all around the edge with a ⅜in (1cm) seam allowance, then snip into the seam allowance all along the curves. Push the backing fabric through the hole to the wrong side of the main piece and press the edges. Topstitch around the edge of the hole about a ¼in (0.6cm) from the edge of the opening. The fabric on the inside can stay loose, but if you'd rather you can use a bit of fusible interfacing to fix it in place.

STEP 4

Cut 2 pieces of fabric from the remnant left in step 1, each 1½ x 12in (4 x 30cm). Fold each in half along the length and then fold the edges under one more time and sew along the edge to close. Fold each loop in half and baste (tack) the ends together at the raw edges. You now have two loops, each about 6in (15cm) long.

STEP 5

Bring the bottom half of the main fabric up and over the section with the hole right sides facing and all the edges aligned, and pin together. Starting along one side near the fold, sew around all three raw edges (if you are using two pieces with no fold, then sew all edges). When you get to the top, place the loops between the layers of fabric, with the loops facing inwards so the raw edges will be sewn into the edge, one at each corner. When the complete edge is sewn, turn the bag right sides out through the hole, and topstitch a ¼in (0.6cm) all around the three sewn sides.

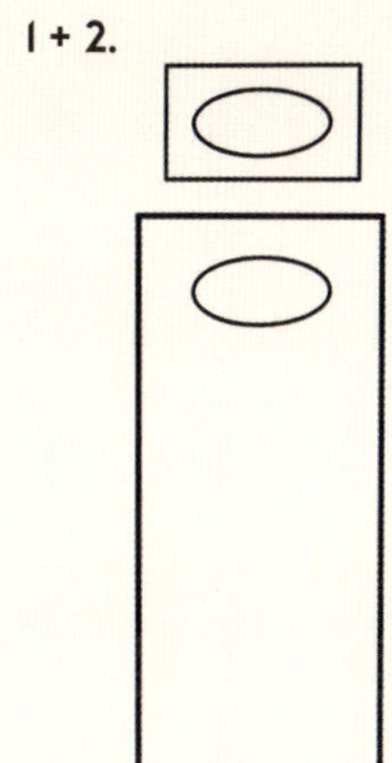

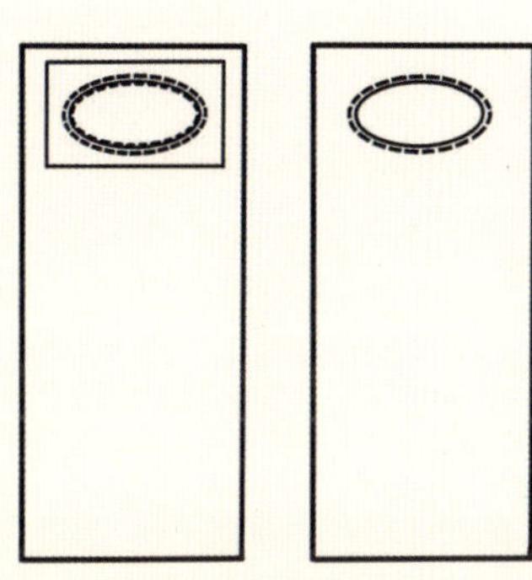

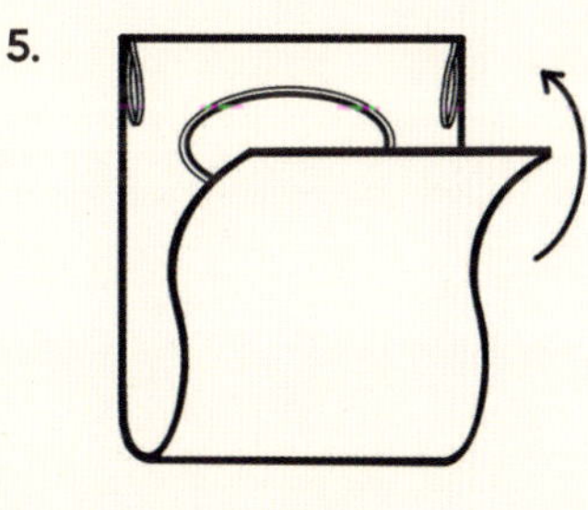

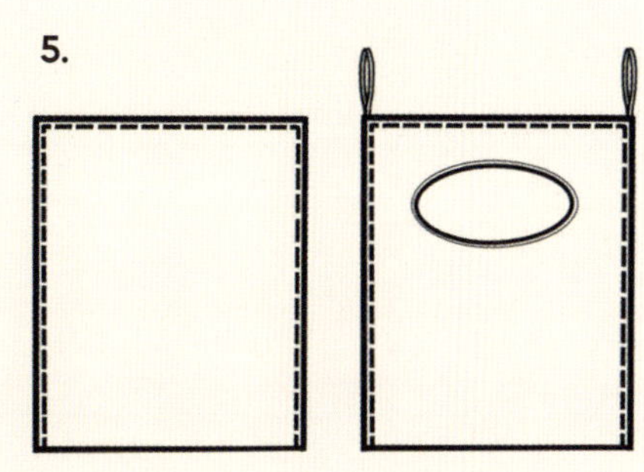

braid-in rag rug

Woven rag rugs can be found anywhere in many different forms and fabrics, from scrap remnants to fine silk. I am partial to this braid-in technique because the strips are woven intertwined with each other so they don't require sewing. Rugs like these always have that wonderful organic quality where different fabrics and colors intermingle with each other. And what better way to reuse clothing that you are no longer wearing. The rug I made is round, but you can adjust the technique slightly to make an oval rug. And while it may seem confusing at first, it really isn't. The key is to work in sequence. With a minimal amount of organizational skill, you'll have no trouble at all. This project works with a variety of fabrics. I used denim, each piece cut to 1in (2.5cm) in width. Starting it is the trickiest part but do your best with your tension and try not to pull it too tight, allowing the piece to lay flat. Try to make sure the fabric tails lay flat and that will give the piece an overall finished look.

What you need

Scraps of fabric such as denim, shirting, and wool
Scissors or rotary cutter and cutting mat
Sewing machine and thread
Safety pins to use as stitch markers
Toothbrush rug needle
Darning needle
Safety pins or crochet hook large enough for the strips (optional)

Finished size

Approx. 36in (91.5cm) diameter

Tips

- If you are using old garments, cut the strips as long as possible, but don't exceed about 40in (101.5cm) because they will be easier to work with if they aren't too long.

- I found it was good to indicate my rows with a safety pin marker so that I had an indication of where to end rows if I wanted to change colors.

- If you find attaching the fabrics using the enclosed join method is not working for you, try hand sewing the pieces together. I found some of the denim I was using was thick and the join was bulky in some areas. Experiment and see which method works best for your piece depending on the fabric you are using.

Instructions

STEP 1

Start by cutting your strips. The width of the strips will determine how chunky you want the rug to be, as will how heavy the fabric is. If you are using thinner fabric such as jersey from old T-shirts, or cotton from shirts or bedding, cut the strips of fabric to about 1½in (4cm) wide. Because I used denim, I found a 1in (2.5cm) width to be fine. It's also a good idea to try to add a few colors rather than do the rug all in one color.

STEP 2

Take three strips and lay them on top of each other just at one end, in any order you wish, with right side facing up and the ends aligned. Using a sewing machine, sew the three strips together right along the ends about ⅛in (0.3cm) from the edge. If the strips are not too thick you can hand sew using a back stitch (see Sewing Techniques: Back Stitch on page 30) if you like.

STEP 3

Working on a table, lay the three strips down flat and slightly separated, and begin by braiding them together to create a standard braid about 4in (10cm) long. Feel free to tape down the sewn end to the table, or use a clipboard if that is easier for you at his point. When you have finished, curl the top of the braid, where you sewed the strips together, downward to form a circle that ends where the braids end. To stabilize the circle, take the strip that is closest to the circle and feed it through one of the braids and then pull it together. If you want to create an oval shape, braid a longer section – 6in (15cm) or more – and rather than forming a circle, keep it straight.

STEP 4

Now you will have a circular shape and three tails. At this point you should add a few more strips so that you end up with at least seven. To do so, take an additional fabric strip in any color you choose, and feed it into one of the braids adjacent to the three working strips, pulling it through about halfway. Feed one more strip into an adjacent braid and you will have seven tails in total.

STEP 5

Start by organizing the seven working strips. For me, because I am right-handed, I have the strips on the right-hand side of the braided circle, extending down towards me, laying flat and side by side – not tangled or overlapping, and in relative order. Keeping the strips ordered will make the weaving less confusing because weaving this kind of rug is about working in sequence, one strip at a time, and always with the strip that is at the outside (right) position. If you want, you can attach a safety pin to the bottom of each strip with a number taped to it going from right to left.

STEP 6

Take the outside strip, in my case the one furthest right, and weave it to the left into the adjacent strips in order, going under and over each one in turn. At the end feed it through the nearest braid in the starting ring, using a tool or needle if necessary. Tighten the weave with your fingers, and pull the strip down, placing it next to the working strips – now it will be laying on the inside, left-hand side in my case.

STEP 7

Repeat this action again, picking up the outside strip (right most), weaving into the adjacent strips, under and over, then anchoring it into the braid, and laying it down on the inside, left side. As you proceed, the braided circle you started with will grow with additional layers. Press the rug flat with your hands as you work and be mindful of not making each weave too tight because then the rug might start to buckle.

STEP 8

Eventually the strips will get shorter as you weave and you will need to lengthen them by joining additional strips. Using an "enclosed join" method such as a no-sew "buttonhole join" works well with most fabrics that aren't too bulky. Cut a small slit about ¾in (2cm) long at the end of the strip you need to lengthen, making no closer than ¼in (0.6cm) from the end. The slit should be vertical – so parallel with the strip. The easiest way is to fold the strip in half and snip, then open up. Make a similar slit on one end of the new strip. Slide the end of the new strip through the slit on the rug, and pull it through a bit. Create a loop by sliding the other end of the new piece through the slit on the new piece and pull until snug. Alternatively, if this doesn't seem suitable for your fabric, you can sew the ends together.

STEP 9

When you get to your desired size, you need to start fastening off to end the braiding. To do this, continue weaving in the same way but rather than pulling the working strip down through the braids, tie it off at that point and snip the tail off. Do the same for each strip in sequence until all strips are attached and clipped.

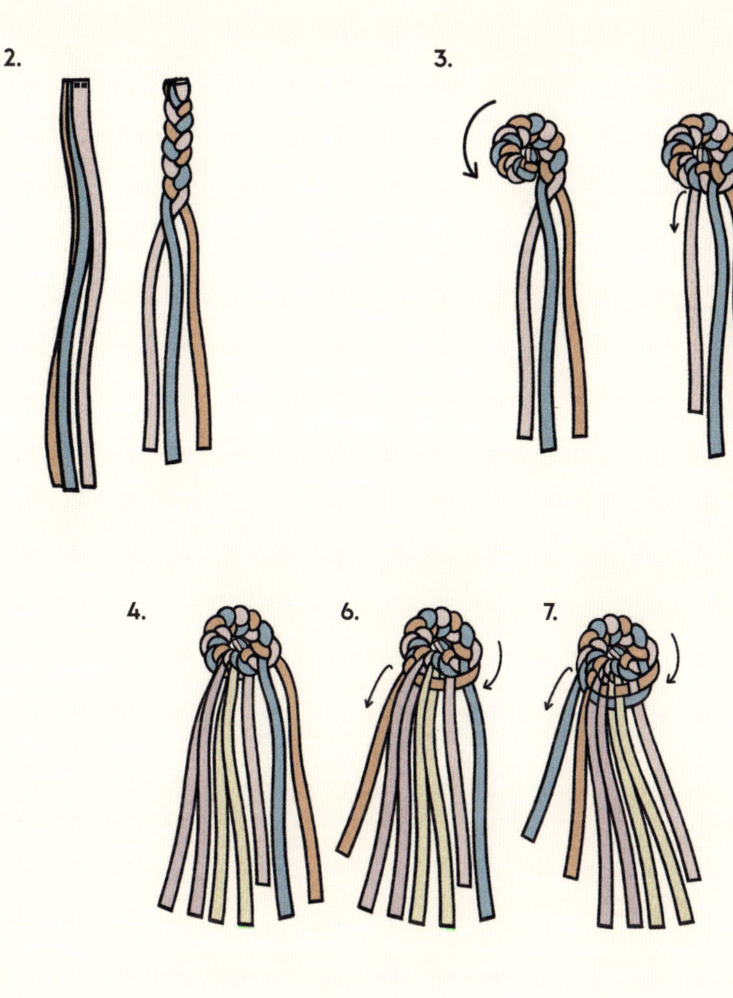
2.
3.
4.
6.
7.

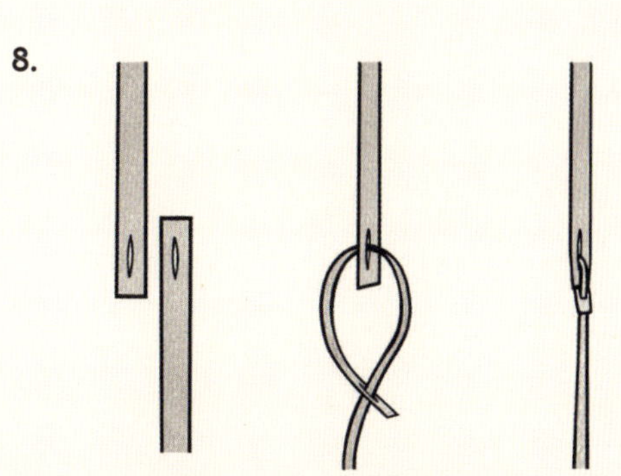
8.

wall hanging/ curtain

This wall hanging is made using a flat-felled seam, which is a centuries-old technique used in clothing and sail making. Because it is finished on both sides with raw edges all concealed, it is used in situations where the item will be unlined. This way of working is also used in Pojagi, a traditional Korean patchwork, which is where I draw my inspiration. It's made by combining all sizes and colors of lightweight remnant fabric that I had on hand. The wall hanging does not need framing – it can hang freely by pinning the corners or you can sew a fabric sleeve on the back for a wooden bar to pass through to hang on the wall. It is also nice as a curtain, with the finished seams having a stained glass quality.

What you need

Approx. 1yd (1m) of fabric in total, use up your remnants
Grid ruler
Water-soluble marker
Rotary knife and cutting mat
Pins
Sewing machine and thread

Finished size

Can be made to any size

Tips

- When arranging the fabrics I find that a common language of horizontals and verticals works well with the occasional odd shape, and is much easier than compositions where everything is different.

- For my composition I typically patched smaller pieces together to create larger blocks, which were then combined to create strips of different sizes. I then combined the strips into the finished composition.

- On one side of the final piece you will have two parallel lines of stitching at each seam, on the other there will only be one line of stitching. These instructions are for two lines on the front – or the right side – of the piece.

- Adding a fabric sleeve along the top of the wall hanging is a nice way to hang it. Cut one long strip the same width or three smaller pieces. Hem the ends, fold the strip in half lengthwise and tuck the two raw edges under the rolled hem at the top in step 6.

Instructions

STEP 1

Start by arranging your fabric remnants on your worktable to find a composition that you are happy with. The layout is entirely up to you, but try working with a random variety of sizes and colors. However, because this project is in many ways about the seams themselves, each piece does not have to be different from its neighbor – I quite often use the same colors next to each other for a more subtle appearance. Don't worry about whether the seams from different blocks or rows line up.

STEP 2

Place two pieces of fabric to be joined wrong sides together one on top of the other. Rather than aligning the raw edges, as you would for simple seams, slide the fabric on top back so that its raw edge is ⅜in (1cm) away from the bottom fabric edge – the edge of the bottom piece will extend beyond the top piece. Make sure this distance is consistent the entire length of the seam. Sew the two pieces together with a stitch line that is about ⅜in (1cm) from the edge of the top piece of fabric.

STEP 3

Next fold the extended bottom edge up and over the edge of the top piece. Pin in place if you like, making sure to keep the fold tight. The raw edge of the top piece is now hidden inside a fold.

STEP 4

Open out your fabric – with both right sides facing up – and fold the seam flat to one side to cover the second raw edge. Pin in place. Stitch the fold down close to the edge along its entire length.

STEP 5

Trim any fabric that extends beyond the seam, and sew another piece to this one, in the same way, continuing until you have made a larger block or row. Join the blocks or rows together, first trimming the edges to be joined so they are straight, and then sewing them together in the same manner.

STEP 6

Finish the outside edge with a rolled hem on all four sides.

acknowledgements

Thank you to everyone at Quadrille Create especially to Oreolu Grillo, Harriet Butt and to Gemma Hayden for designing a beautiful book. Thank you also to Marie Clayton for editing my words and to John Booth for all the illustrations and diagrams.

Thank you to Kim Lightbody for photographing the book, it was wonderful seeing my projects through your eyes and to Milly Bruce for her styling work and eye for detail.

To all the people who support me from near and far, my dear friends, my amazing mum, Sengchanh, and the Booths, and all of you who follow my process on social media – your positive energy makes my every day brighter.

To my children, Lliam and Piper, you two are my heart and I love you both dearly.

A big thank you and lots of love to John for your endless support in life and business and for helping me make sense of my words; without you by my side none of this would be possible xx

1
4
13
11
20
17
11
18
9
8
6
19
7
14
16
13
10
5
12
RotaTrim A3
3
2
15

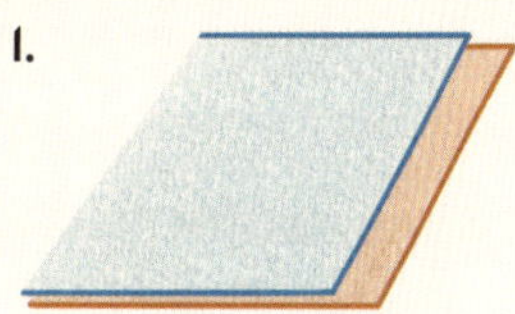

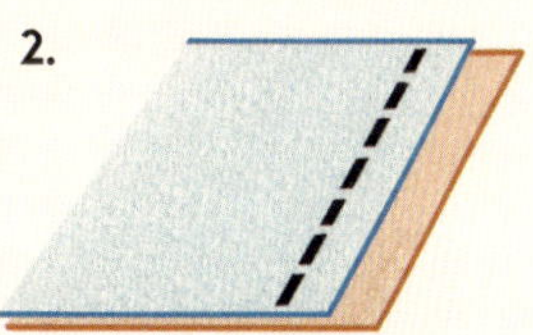

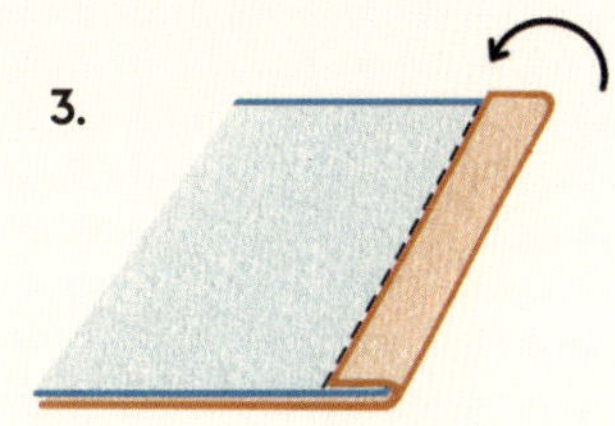

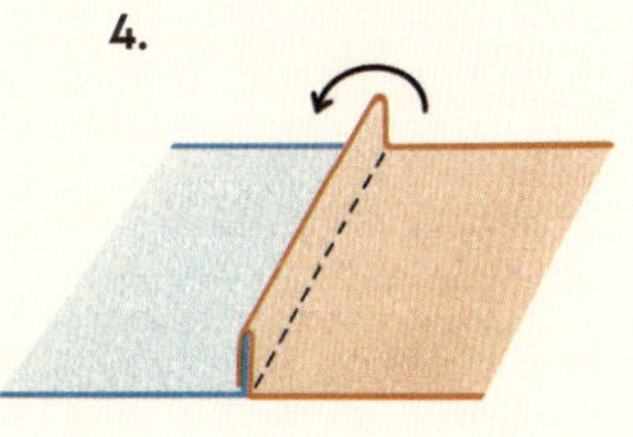

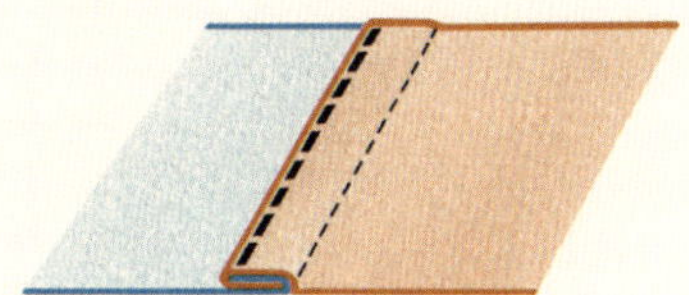

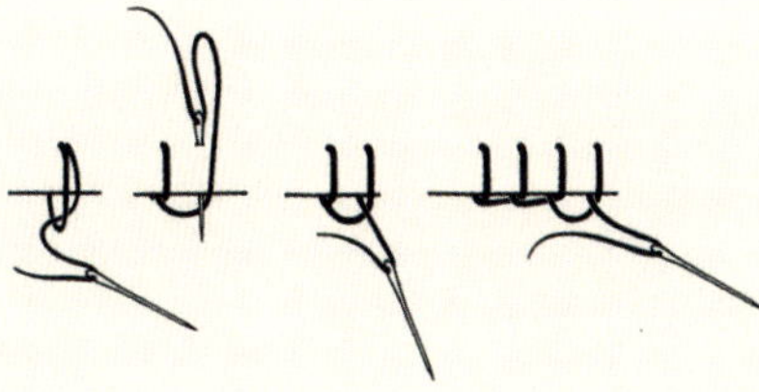

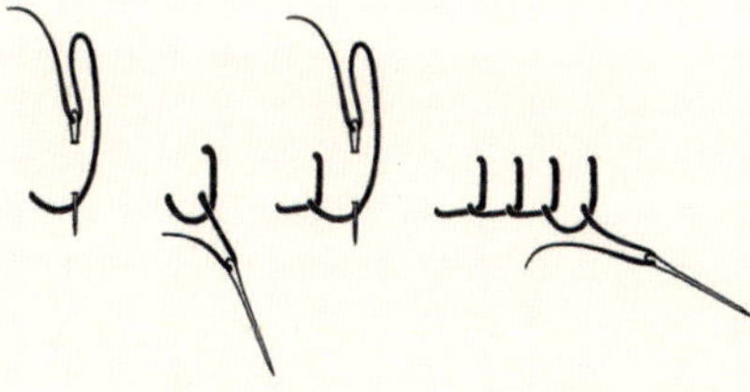

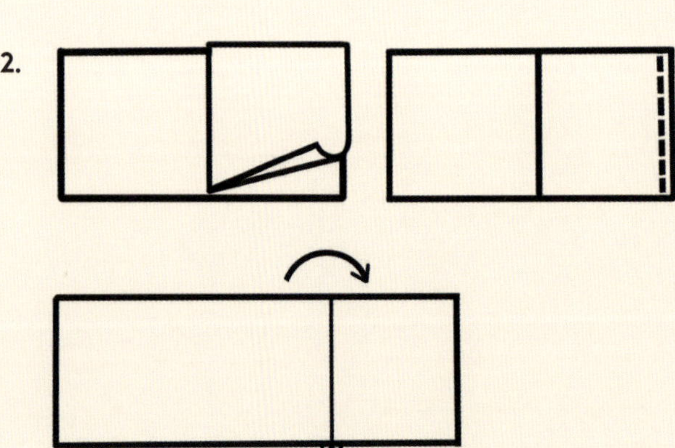

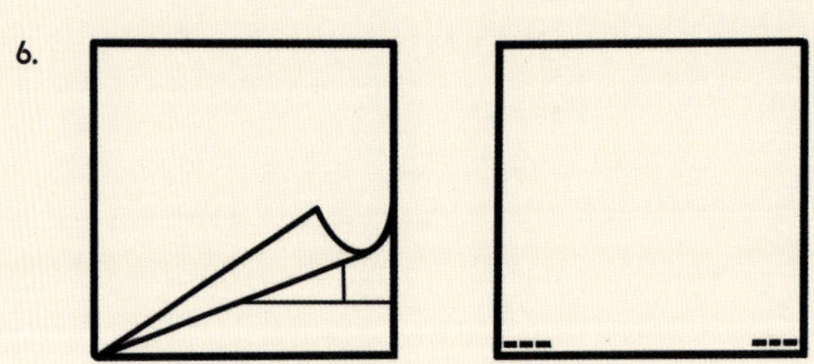

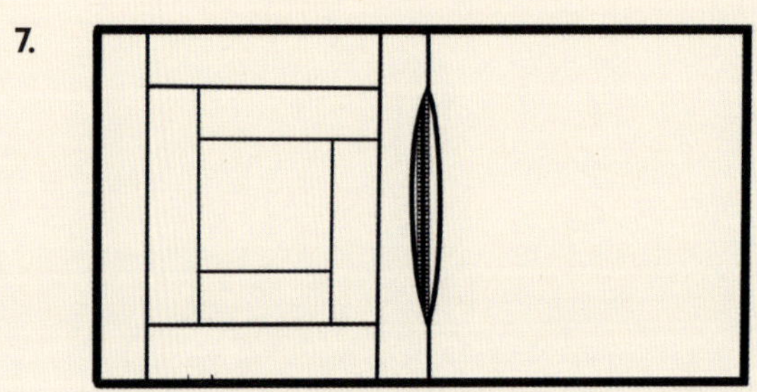

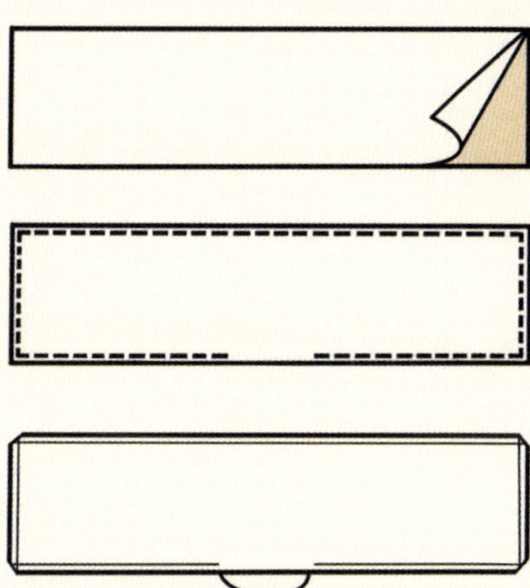

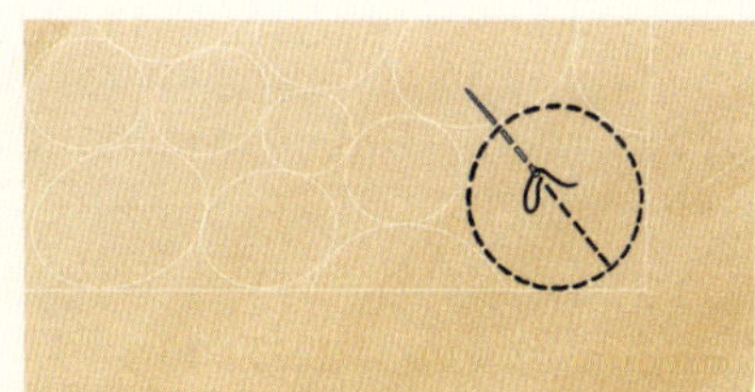

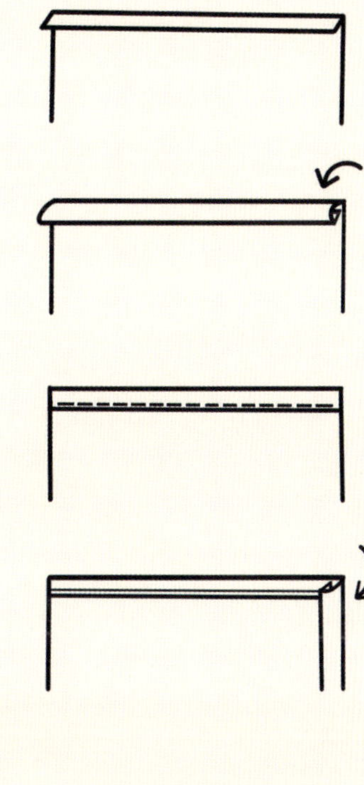

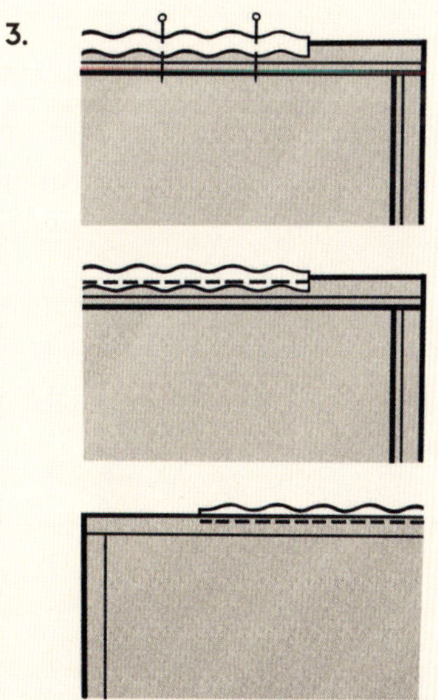

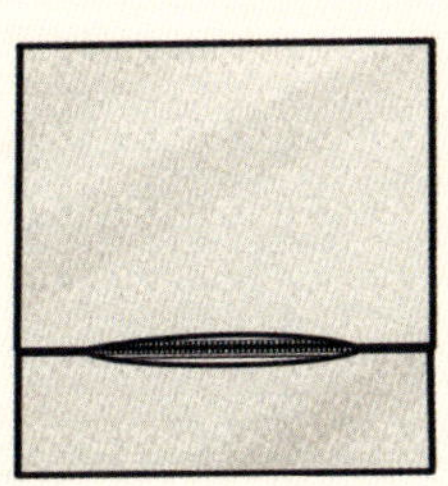

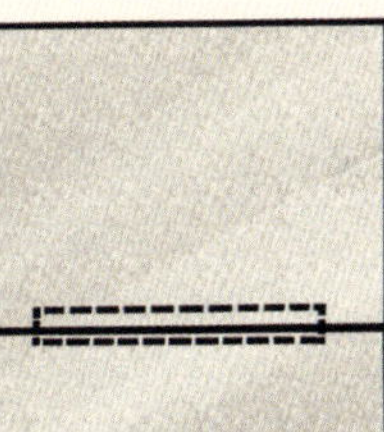

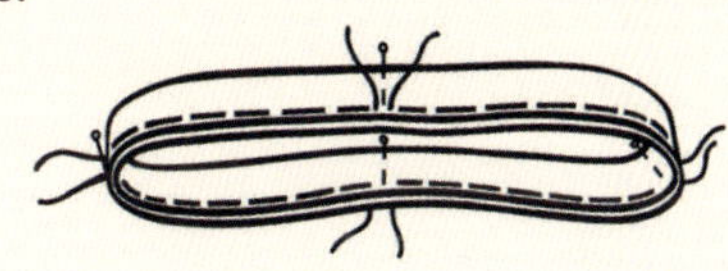

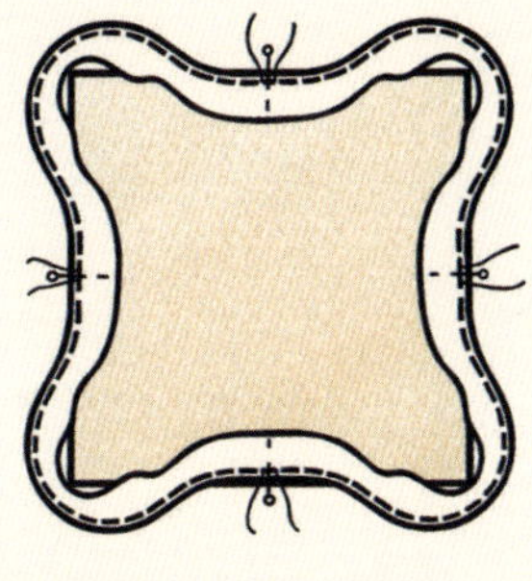

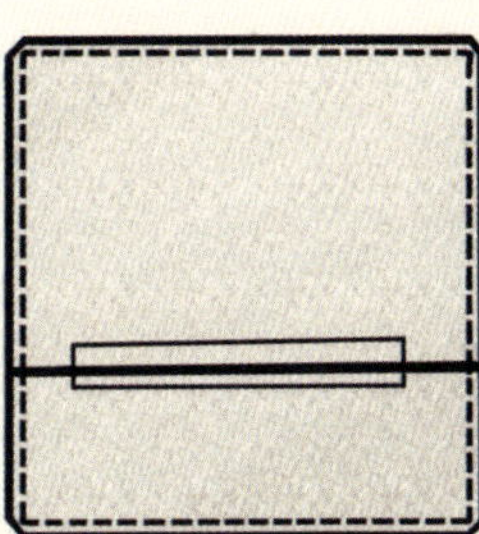

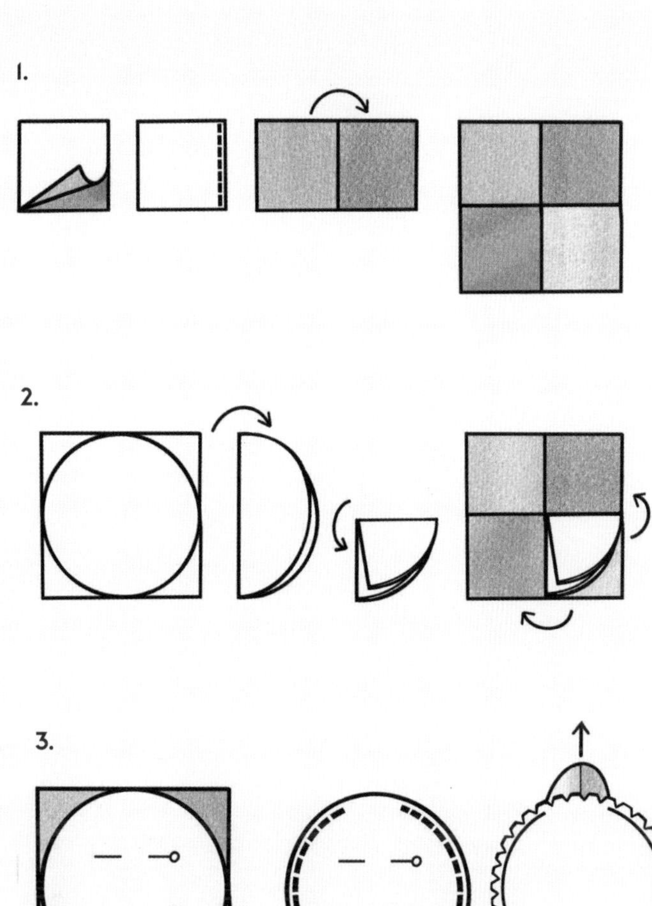

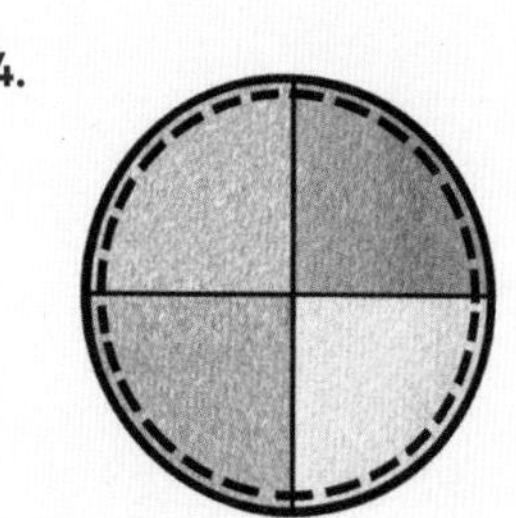

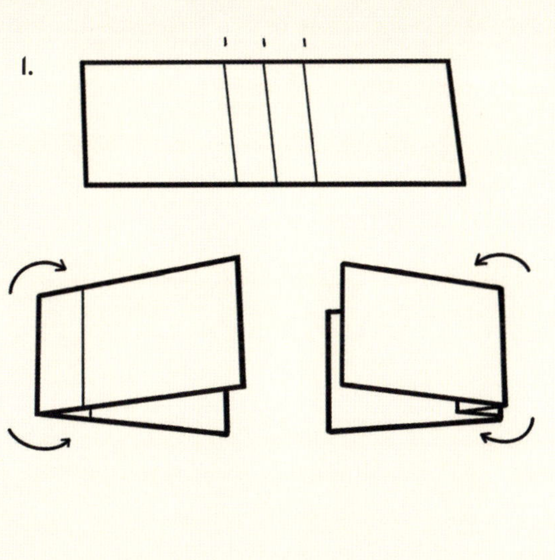

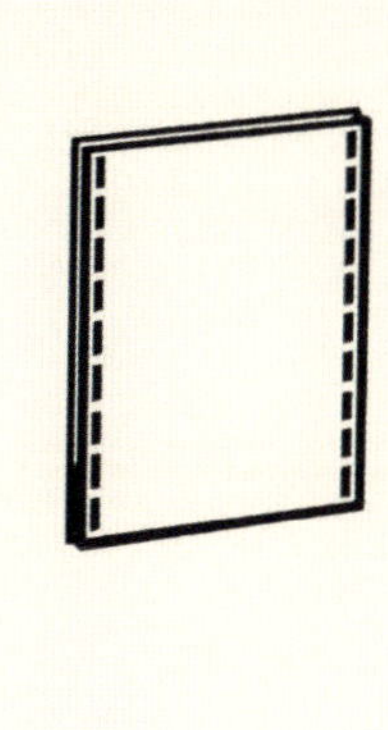

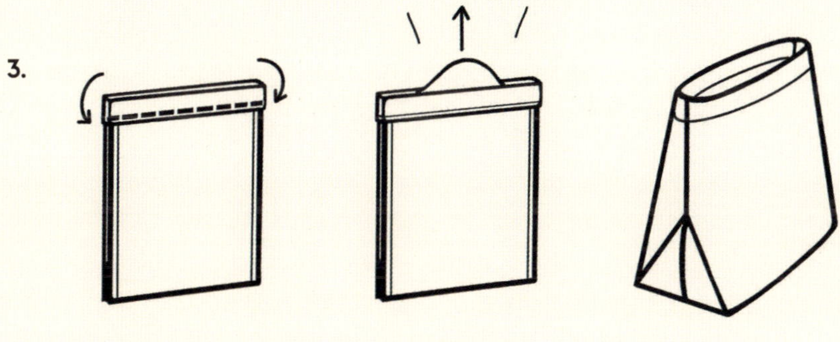

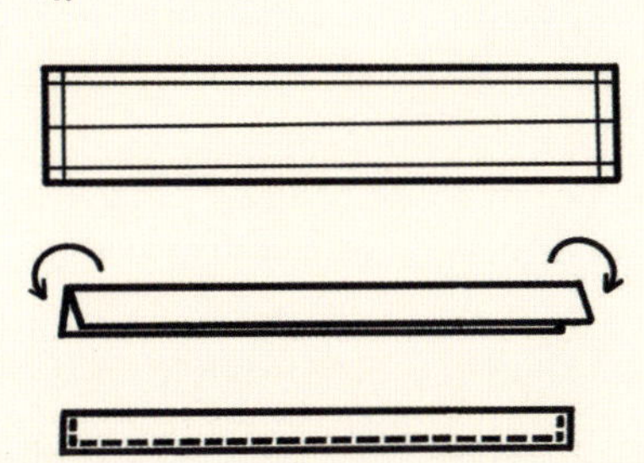

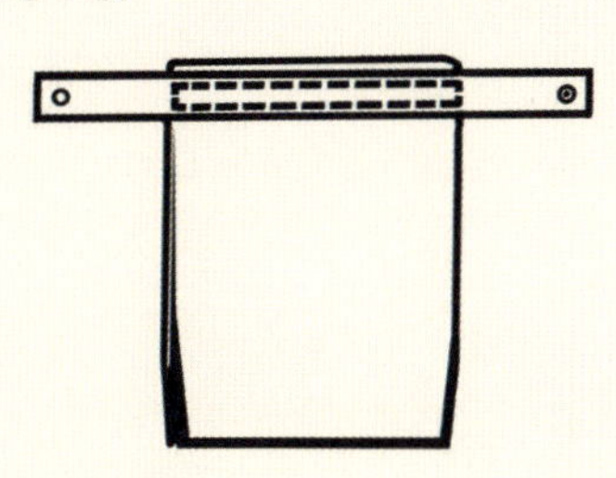

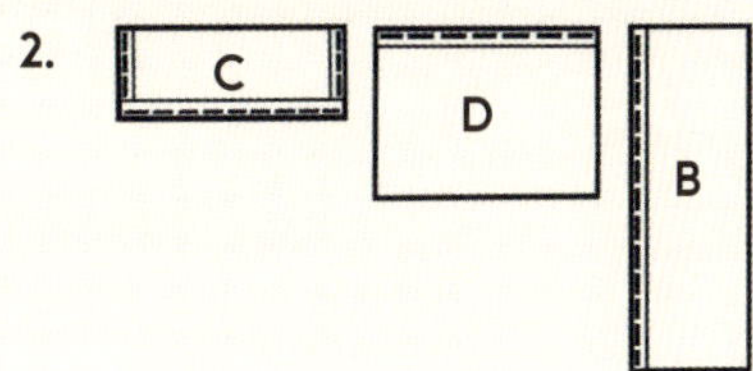

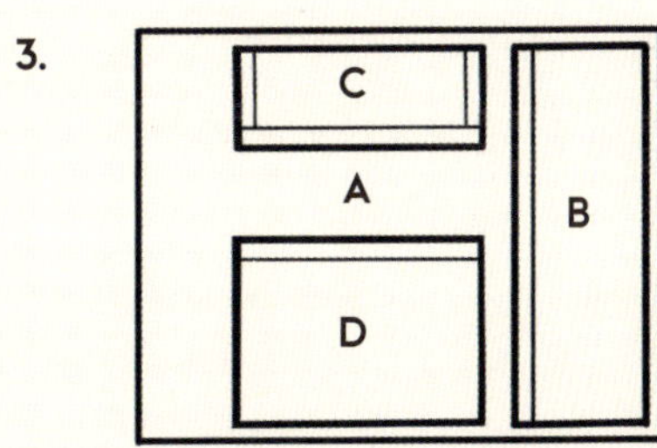

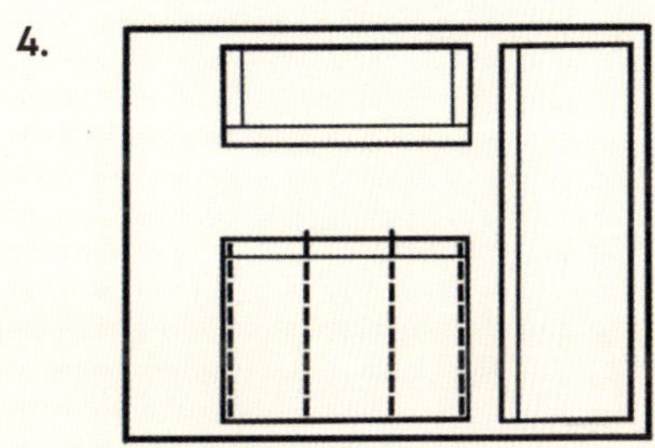

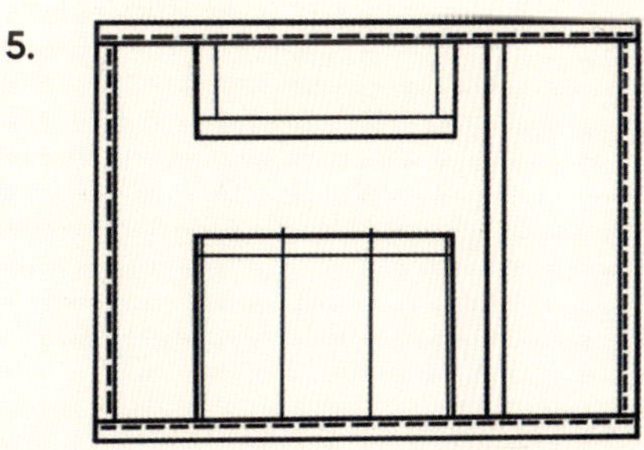

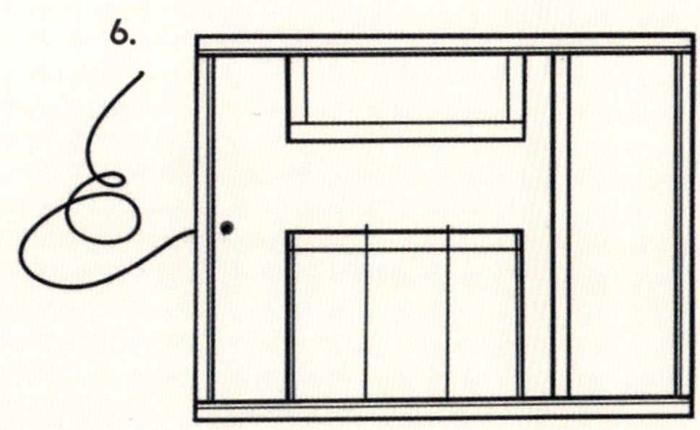

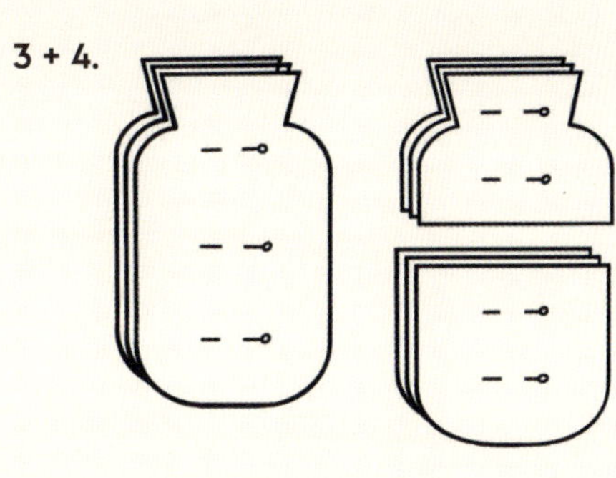

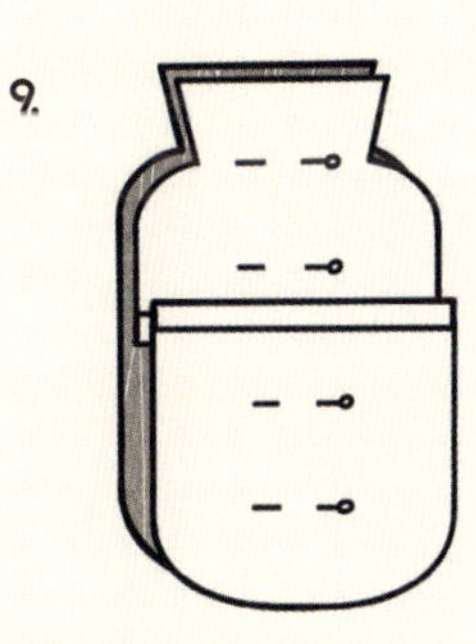

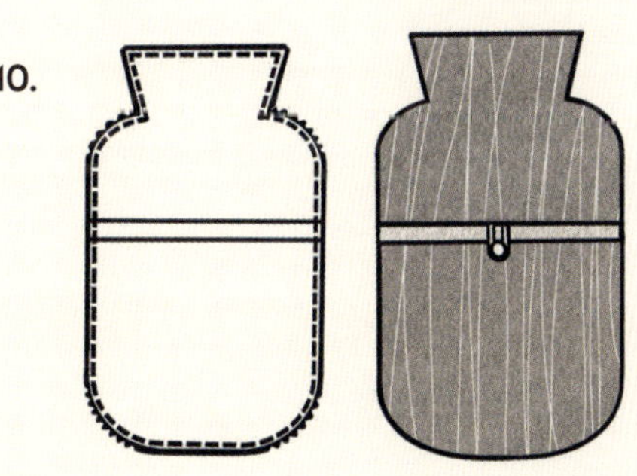

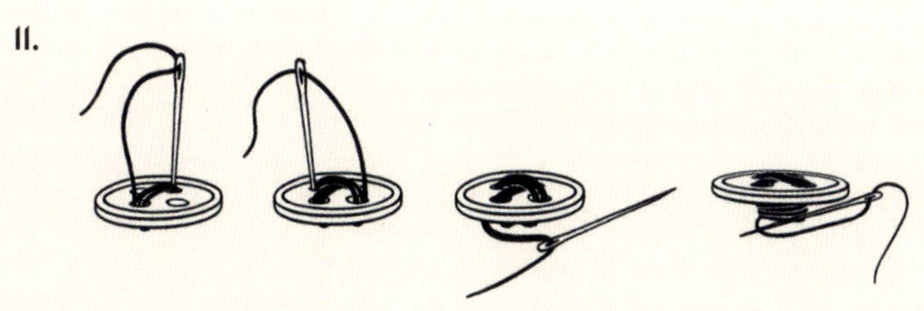

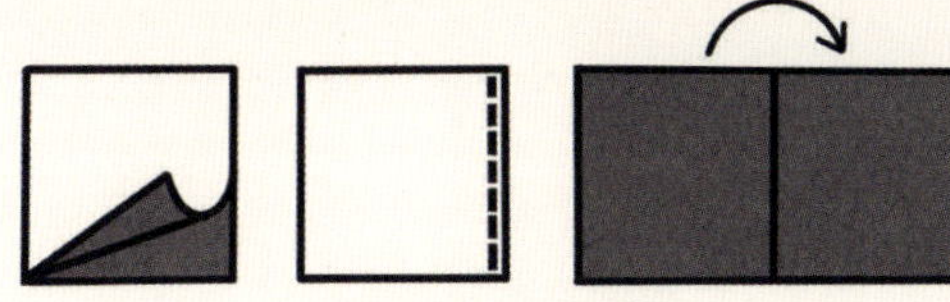

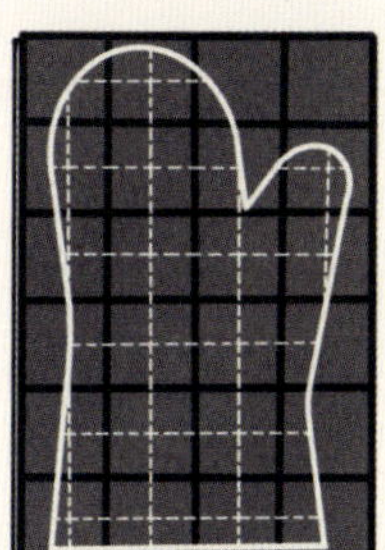

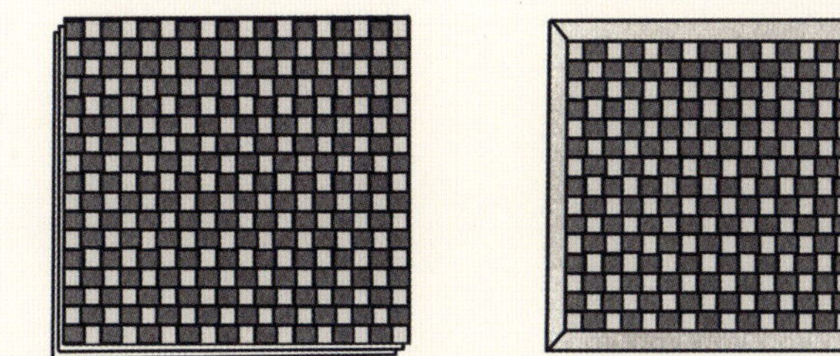

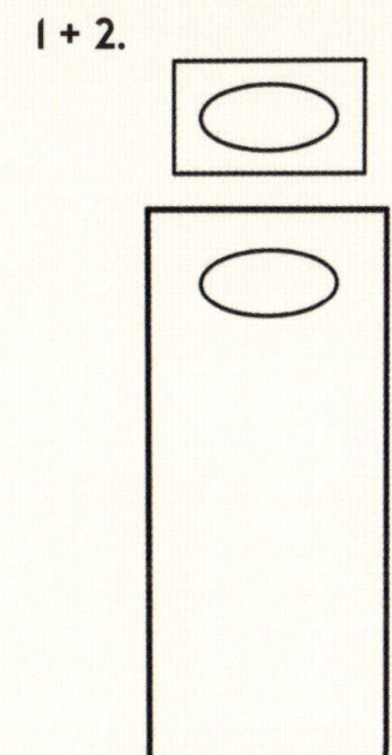

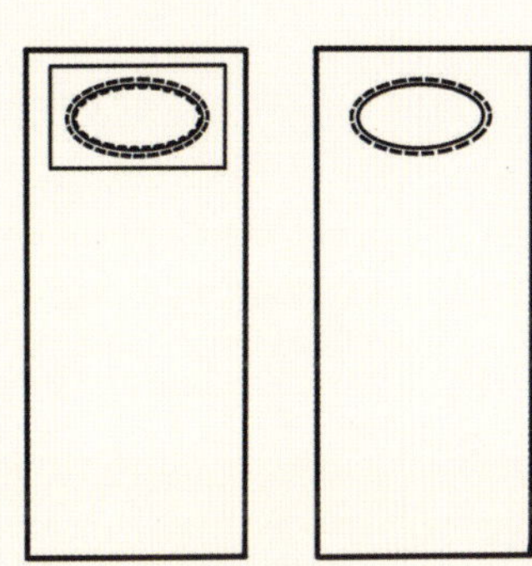

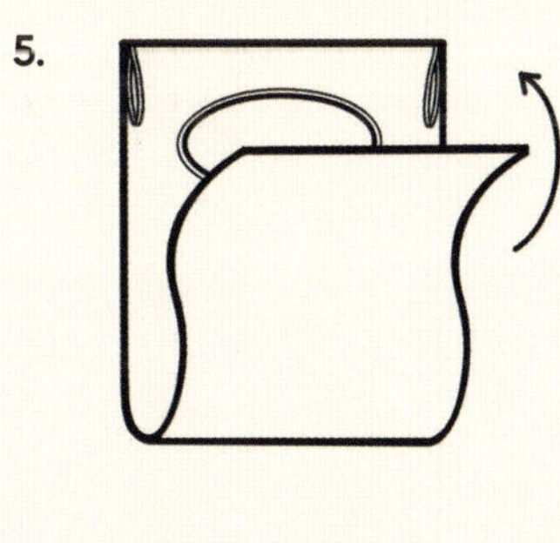

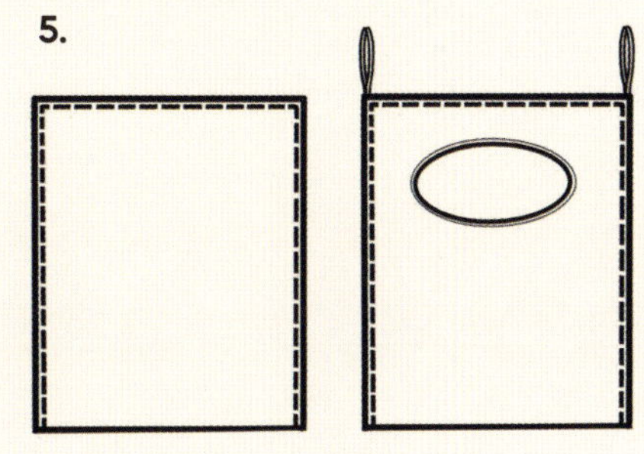

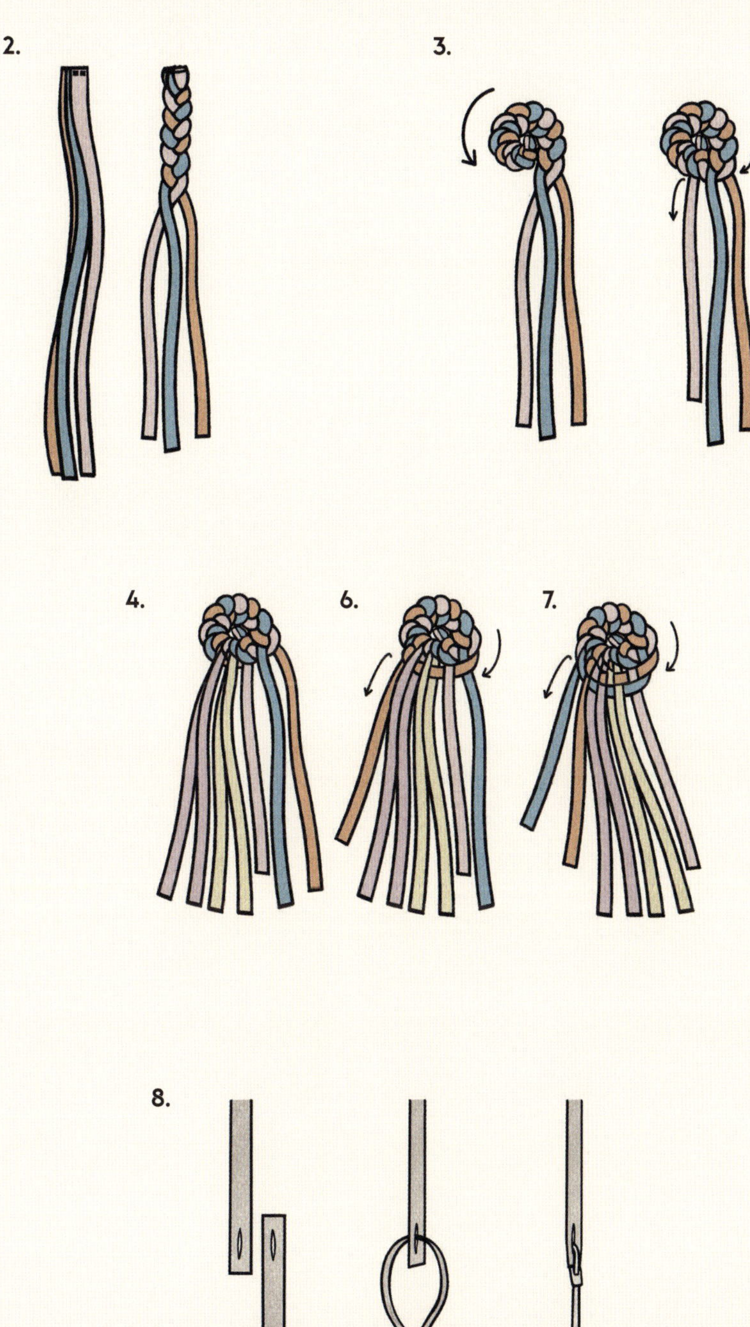